Rhymes & Reasons

The Art of Writing Poetry

— TOBY WREN —

Wren Press Books
81 Rivington Street, London, EC2A 3AY
www.wrenpressbooks.com
enquiries@wrenpressbooks.com

Copyright © Toby Wren 2015

*This book may not be copied or otherwise reproduced either
wholly or in part without prior written permission from the author.
It is sold subject to the condition that it shall not,
by way of trade or otherwise, be lent, resold, hired out
or otherwise circulated in any form of binding or cover
other than that in which it is published and without
a similar condition including this condition being
imposed on the subsequently purchaser.*

All rights reserved.

*First published in France in March 2011 by
Wren Press as a limited first edition.*

This revised edition published 2015.

Poetry is an art, and like any other form of personal expression, the would-be writer must first be gifted with an ability to write. An initial spark of inspiration must exist...it cannot be taught.

The best that this book or any other can hope to achieve, therefore, is to provide guidance into various styles and techniques of writing, which may well enhance an inherent talent.

The second important thing (implicit in the original book title) is my belief that writing poetry should be an activity designed to provide an element of achievement and fun.

Information provided in this book is intended to emphasise this approach. Writing poetry may well be challenging, occasionally frustrating, and often exciting. It will not always be easy - although few things worth doing are ever easy. However, when the final line of the poem is written, there should always be a sense of satisfaction...of having found a voice.

For many writers, myself included, it will become apparent that writing is not always something we may consciously choose to do: it is more true to say that writing is something we are simply unable not to do. A sense of compulsion is necessary, therefore, combined with an ability to observe and experience everything around... to cogitate and think great thoughts, and to then express all of this in some original, emotional and personal manner.

I feel that a final observation is needed whenever mention is made of rules or techniques in writing poetry, particularly with regard to the more traditional forms of construction. Rules can be broken, and no technique should ever be allowed to restrict or smother the art of poetry. It is better that the structure bends to suit the poem, rather than any attempt to wedge the poem into a recognised format.

This is not to suggest that guidelines should be disregarded at the first hint of a challenge, but where this is seen to make dull some aesthetic quality of the poem, then better always that it should be allowed to shine.

Introduction

In 1983 I wrote a book "**Poetry For Fun**" (*ISBN 0 907820 24 7*). It was a modest publication of just 40 pages, and was intended mainly for members of a writers' circle who had requested a brief beginner's guide into the art of writing poetry. It was to become more successful than I had anticipated, with two reprints and interest that extended beyond my immediate circle of friends.

I doubt whether more than a few books survive today, although from my own somewhat well-thumbed copy, it seems that the information provided was helpful. It was also apparent that this early book might be expanded to encompass a greater range of information on the writing of poetry, with additional items and a more comprehensive range of topics.

The new book "**Rhymes & Reasons**" was five times larger than the previous guide, and had grown somewhat alarmingly to include a range of new ideas. I had also set myself the task of writing all poems included in the book, many of which were specifically intended to illustrate various forms of poetry... a somewhat daunting challenge in itself. The book was later published as a limited first edition by Wren Press in 2011.

More recently, a further revision of the book has taken place to review existing topics and expand slightly on a few more. These additional changes have been prompted also by a decision to make the book available to a wider readership.

A few significant points were made in the previous books, and I feel it would be as well to remind ourselves of these.

The first important observation I would make is that it is not possible to teach anyone how to become a poet. There are many books that suggest there is some secret charm by which this may be achieved...it is not so.

Oriental Poetry:	237
Japanese Poetry:	239
haiku, tanka, naga-uta, renga	240
renga chain, haiku no renga, senryu	244
modern haiku.	245
Chinese Poetry:	246
t'ang, shi, ku-shi, lü-shi	246
jinti-shi, tz'u, xin-shi	247
Korean Poetry:	249
sijo verse	249
Final Words	251
Index	257
Alphabetical Index of Poems	259
Meters Summary List	265
Alphabetical Index of Key Words	267
Alphabetical Index of Poets	275

Contents

Introduction	11
Making A Start	15
Poetry and Verse	17
Stress and Accent	27
Use of Meter	32
Use of Rhyme	60
Use of Words	73
Length of Lines	97
Stanza Forms	105
Traditional Poetry:	147
Sonnets	149
Ballads and Ballades	165
Rondels, Rondeaus, Roundels	173
Rondelets and Roundelays	
Triolet, Villanelle, Pantoum	179
Curtal Sonnet , Kyrielle, Lai	184
Ode, Epic Poem, Elegy, Sestina	188
Greek Poetry	193
Welsh Poetry - Awdl Gywydd	194
Modern Poetry:	197
Acrostic, Telestich, Alphabetical	199
Mixed Meter, Logaoedic, Macaronic	205
Comedy - Pastiche, Parody, Lampoon	208
Playing with Words:	215
Limerick and Clerihew	217
Rhopalic Verse, Cinquains, Triversan	220
All Shapes and Sizes:	223
Spatial and Concrete Poetry	225
Calligrammes	226
Vanishing Sonnet, Nonet, Minute	230
Etheree, Twin Etheree	234

Dedication

This book is dedicated to those for whom
the writing of poetry is a compulsion and a delight.
May it ever remain so.

Acknowledgements

I wish to thank many friends and family
for their encouragement and constructive criticism.
Not that I needed much encouragement
when it came to writing poetry, which has been an abiding
interest over the past half century.

Many long-standing friendships have been made during this time,
together with the exchange of ideas
and the sharing of many fine poems.
To one and all I convey my sincere appreciation
for all of this.

My wife, Nancy, and our children, Claire and James,
have been a constant source of inspiration.
Their honest appreciation of what is or is not a worthy poem
has been of paramount importance
in honing whatever skills I have.
Proof-reader extraordinaire...
it is finally with Nancy's help and encouragement
and that of my son, James,
during the final stages of preparation
that this book has been completed.

RHYMES & REASONS

It is said that a poem is never finished...it is abandoned. In the same way as the artist must decide on his last brush-stroke, so too must the poet decide when to leave the poem and move on. A technique favoured by myself, in fact, is to complete a first draft and then allow time to "mature" before considering any further "tinkering"... and even then only if absolutely sure of any changes needed.

Poetry is both a visual and an oral expression of thought, and I often find it useful at this stage to read the poem aloud, and judge whether it sounds right.

I have, as far as possible, arranged for poems included in this book to be placed adjacent to the various topics they are intended to illustrate. In some instances, however, when writing these poems I have attempted to cover more than one aspect, so they may appear near one topic, whilst at a distance from another. An alphabetical index of poems, therefore, includes references to one or more aspects that the poems may serve to show. An alphabetical index of key words used in poetry is also provided.

By word and example then, it is hoped that this book will provide rhymes and reasons for writing poetry, along with a greater degree of depth and understanding of this art.

Toby Wren
June 2015

MAKING A START

Poetry and Verse

Historical Background

Poetry has its origins in verbal communication, ancient sagas and the like, from a time of recorded events through ballads and performance poetry. The use of strong meter and rhyme introduced a musical quality to such recitals, as well as aiding remembrance at a time that predated literacy.

Ancient civilised societies (and in particular the Greeks) subsequently developed poetry into 'traditional' formats of structure and presentation.

Poetry

"The best words in the best order" as expressed by Samuel Taylor Coleridge (1772 - 1834)

Poetry is an elevated use of words and language with succinct expression, often presented in a classical or organised format (such as the sonnet or villanelle) although this does not preclude less structured writing, such as free verse. The poem should aim to show originality in terms of personal views and thoughts.

Verse

All poetry is verse, but not all verse is poetry. The distinction lies in the realisation that verse is generally regarded as being of a simpler construction, with looser control of words and phrases. This is still able to portray strong emotions, usually in a direct and easily recognised manner.

However, verse lacks the depth of poetry, often discovered by the use of metaphor, which appears to describe one thing whilst actually expressing some more profound meaning. Simple verse, however, does have a public appeal and is found in items such as greetings cards. It is often what most folk think of as poetry, and this is no bad thing.

Note: A poem is not made up of verses. These are stanzas.

Vers Libre

More commonly known as "free verse", although this is a misnomer since "vers libre" is actually poetry not verse, and is seen in a form which has abandoned traditional meter or rhyme in favour of natural rhythm. This liberal idea was first introduced during the late 19th century by poets such as Arthur Rimbaud (1854 - 1891), and has gained wide-spread acceptance in modern times.

Blank Verse

Blank verse is also non-rhyming poetry, but has a retained meter. This can add structure to the poem and will often include a sense of movement.

Prose Poem

The prose poem is a free verse format with a loose and random structure, although to work as poetry it must also have a "charged" descriptive use of language. This will often include a strong use of meter and sense of flow, and may include random rhyme as well as use of assonance and alliteration.

Doggerel

Doggerel is seen as a poor quality form of verse, lacking depth or emotional impact and often produced by writers with no true appreciation of what poetry is intended to achieve.

"If it rhymes it must be poetry" is seen to be a blatantly misguided statement and clearly untrue.

Doggerel may often show a frequent disregard of any conflict between word accent and line stress (which we will look at later) and may include forced rhyme with words that seem trite and clichéd. The work and dubious reputation of William Topaz McGonagall (1825 - 1902) is frequently cited when describing doggerel.

Examples

Let us look at a few examples of what has been said. Consider, for instance, a simple nursery rhyme. Most nursery rhymes appear at first glance to be amusing with hints of fantasy about them.

GOOSEY, GOOSEY GANDER

Goosey, goosey gander, whither do you wander?
Upstairs, downstairs, in my lady's chamber.
There I met an old man who wouldn't say his prayers,
So I took him by the left leg and threw him down the stairs.

Hardly the sort of behaviour one might want to encourage in children. However, most nursery rhymes were actually written as anonymous statements of social, historical and often political comment at the time, which may serve to explain the subsequent obscurity of their meaning.

This example was written at the time of Oliver Cromwell and the searching out of Royalists opposed to Protestant rule, where the old man would have been a Catholic priest (who would not have said his prayers in a Protestant church) found in hiding during a search of the home of a Royalist "lord and lady".

As a rhyme, it is of simple construction with a strong sense of meter, and is therefore easily remembered and repeated.

Modern Poetry

Modern poetry is often written in free verse, which lacks both rhyme and meter, but has a brevity of expression that provides a degree of added impact. Some unexpected turn of phrase or idea may help us remember it, and our expectation will be that the poem should provide some depth of meaning from the few words used to express an emotion.

SMALL WONDER

Small wonder,
when it took till morning
to say goodnight...

it would take a lifetime
to say goodbye.

In the above poem, sentiments are expressed using everyday words and natural speech, although it is not the literal statement that holds any true meaning. The use of metaphor, as we will come to discover, adds depth and layers of meaning to the poem.

Robert Lee Frost (1874 - 1963), (one of the greatest 20th century poets in my view), once said:

> *"Poetry begins in trivial metaphors, pretty metaphors, 'grace' metaphors, and goes on to the profoundest thinking that we have. Poetry provides the one permissible way of saying one thing and meaning another.... Unless you are at home in the metaphor, unless you have had your proper poetical education in the metaphor, you are not safe anywhere."*

It is this use of metaphor, and the ability to create layers of meaning that elevates the poem above the more obvious and simple verse. This is not to say, however, that verse cannot sometimes include a great depth of emotion.

Similarly, we may sometimes come across some brief paragraph or statement in an book or article, which (unintentionally) by its very nature may also be seen as poetry requiring little, if any, modification. This is known, appropriately enough, as a "found poem". It is a lesson learnt, that poetry may be found in the most unlikely of circumstances.

Prose Poem

A prose poem is similar to free verse in many ways, but will often include the use of language to create descriptive images and a general atmosphere. This may be presented in lines of irregular length, or sometimes as simple paragraphs, but always with some hidden depth.

In the example that follows, we may notice how the prose poem lacks any sense of meter and how the lines of the poem occur at intervals of natural phrasing. This encourages us to take brief pauses, allowing descriptive images to build into an overall effect. The length of lines could, of course, be longer, but short lines seem appropriate for the example shown. Such brief glimpses of nature are sometimes described appropriately enough as a "pen-pictures".

> ***BEAUTY***
>
> *The sound of bird-song*
> *in a cathedral of soft, green shadows.*
>
> *Mottled sunlight*
> *splashing to forest floor*
> *in puddles of dappled gold.*
>
> *The glimmer of water*
> *sliding over polished stone,*
> *where a turquoise dragonfly*
> *patrols the silver stream.*
>
> *All this...and time*
> *to wander, undisturbed,*
> *the halcyon path of beauty.*

An alternative method sometimes employed when writing prose is to divide the poem into lines according to the number of syllables in each. This too creates a fairly natural effect, although there will still be additional (mid-line) pauses that need to be taken.

Lines of approximately equal length (if not precisely defined by counting syllables) may also show a series of natural pauses.

GEOGRAPHY OF UNDERSTANDING

Geography and history divide us
and permutations of desire
are beyond my arithmetic.

Heartache evades biology:
scientific formulae
cannot extrapolate for me
the energy of passion.

I know only of love:
translated into the language
of time and distance

which measures your having left –
and my waiting to follow you.

Blank verse is a popular modern form of poetry, combining as it does a freedom from rhyme, yet retaining a strict meter, which becomes apparent. The meter and length of lines may vary, but will follow a uniform pattern throughout each individual poem.

In an example that follows an iambic pentameter has been used. The iambic meter is a popular choice, since it is akin to natural speech and also provides lines of a moderate length, thereby adding a natural cadence to the flow of words

We will look at the types of meter later, but suffice for now to note that this has a steady accent on every second syllable. In future notes I intend to employ a phonetic illustration of unstressed and stressed syllables using the convention shown:

*ti-**TUM**, ti-**TUM**, ti-**TUM** ti-**TUM** ti-**TUM***

THE WAY OF THINGS

Another Day...

It is the way of things – it does not change.
The church bell tolls the early morning hour
to rouse the sleepy village once again.

Already risen, like his crusty loaves,
the baker opens wide his doors, to send
the wafts of fresh-baked bread into the street.

A tractor passes by... an early start
to plough the fields before the eventide.
Another day, steeped in the country ways

of crops and seasons, and the heritage
of rural life and agricultural lore.
It is the way of things – it does not change.

Market Day...

Another mid-week market day arrives.
The village comes alive with busy noise
to rouse the sleepy streets, nor heed the clock

which tolls un-noticed on this sunny day.
The high street closed, is crowded now with stalls
of local fruit and vegetables still fresh

with morning dew where, but an hour before,
they waited to be taken from the fields.
A day when all folk come to sell and buy –

perhaps bright ribbons for a summer dress,
or cheese and flour, and some local wine.
Another mid-week market day arrives.

Late Afternoon...

Late afternoon, when old men sit and talk
of days recalled when they had work to do,
and crops to harvest from the distant fields.

No more for them such tasks – their sturdy sons
have taken up the yoke of labour now.
A time when old men seek the café shade

to sip a demitasse of coffee there:
thin, fragile handles delicately pinched
so gently in their rough and calloused hands.

The church bell tolls another passing hour:
it is the way of things – it does not change.
Late afternoon, when old men sit and talk.

It will be seen that the poem has three distinct sections and moves slowly through a typical day in some sleepy French village. The use of a refrain line at the start and finish of each section of this poem is also fairly obvious, and in this instance has been done to achieve a "rounding-off" effect. Refrain lines can also be used to great effect, as we will come to see.

It is usual to employ a uniform meter when writing blank verse, thereby achieving a steady passage of words. The mixing of meters is also possible, and can quicken or slow the pace in places for added effect, as will be shown later. However, some care is required to ensure that the poem retains a continuous flow throughout, rather than assuming the less smooth structure of free verse.

It would hardly seem to be of any particular benefit to include an example of doggerel, having established that this is something we wish studiously to avoid. However, there are lessons to be learnt from mistakes seen in things done incorrectly, as well as those gained from examples that we wish to emulate.

THE POOR BIRD

A bird sat high up in a tree
and sang as happy as could be,
when suddenly a cat came by
and saw the bird perched up so high.

The cat jumped up to grab the bird.
A lot of squawking could be heard.
The cat had hurt the poor bird's wing,
which was a truly awful thing.

Away the frightened bird then flew,
though where it went nobody knew.
The cat just looked and walked away,
in search of something else to play.

What can we say that is good about this poem? It has a steady meter and rhyming couplets, although a frequent criticism of such construction is the inclusion of inversions, where the words of a normal sentence are re-arranged to achieve a "sledge-hammer" rhyme.

"Away the frightened bird then flew" creates a stilted effect, and leaves little poetry for us to find.

It is important to ensure that poetry is written in a way that makes best use of correct grammar in the construction of sentences. It should also reflect modern use of English and not adopt any affectations of flowery expression or use of archaic words, as we shall see later.

In the case of free verse, this can appear as quite a normal way of speaking, which (on the surface) may not strongly hint at poetry at all. The following poem is intended to show this approach. With these early observations in mind, we can now begin to look at lines of poetry and various types of meter.

HOW EASY IT WAS

*How easy it was
in the green years of my awareness
to write of love.*

*Ignorance makes heroes of us all:
stumbling over words
whilst seeking some meaning to emotions.*

*Love or desire?
It is difficult, sometimes,
to see the candle that shines against the sun.*

*And it has become no easier now
with the fading vision of age
to write of love:
to understand such true meaning.*

*Easier, perhaps, to speak of friendship
and the comfort of our lives together.*

*Easier to touch a shared understanding
with that same softness of thought
as when I might touch your body.*

*And is this love?
To embrace, warm and naked:
to escape the harsh truth of loneliness.*

*A harmony of emotions, perhaps,
and the dreams we must seek together,
or never seek at all.*

Stress and Accent

Historical Background

The tradition of ancient poetry depended for its dramatic effect on the use of a strong meter. This would not only carry the story along, but could be varied in much the same way as the drum beat of primitive percussion music, to create drama and variation.

This is as true today as it was in the past.

Accent

All words of more than one syllable will have an accent: an emphasis on part of the word at some natural position, in keeping with normal conversation. Longer words may well include a need for more than one accentuated part.

For example:

The words "shining" and "brightly" have two syllables and are spoken as "**shi**-ning" and "**bright**-ly" with the emphasis (accent) on the start of the words.

The emphasis (em-**pha**-sis) may come at any part of the word, but will always be spoken as we would expect it to be which is hardly sur-**pris**-ing.

Stress

When we come to write a line of poetry with a defined meter, we start to introduce stresses along its length. There are many recognised forms of meter, which we will look at later, and the controlled mixing of meters may also be used to great effect.

The important thing to recognise, however, is that once a meter has been established, it should flow in a continuous manner, and will often dominate what is being said in order to do so.

Harmony

The combination of line stress and word accent will most often live happily together, since there is a natural tendency to compose poetry in a way that sounds right.

So we might then write:

>The stars were shining brightly in the night
>*(The **stars** were **shi**ning **bright**ly **in** the **night**)*

This harmony of unstressed and stressed syllables is clearly shown using the phonetic convention as previously mentioned:

>*ti-**TUM**, ti-**TUM**, ti-**TUM** ti-**TUM** ti-**TUM***

There is a temptation sometimes when writing poetry to assume an "poetical tone" in what is being described, which is quite alien to normal conversation. This is seen occasionally in classical poetry, written in what was thought to be a scholarly and acceptable form of expression at the time. However, modern poetry tends to communicate in a more clear and concise manner, rather than making use of any archaic words.

Looking again at our line

>The stars were shining brightly in the night
>*(The **stars** were **shi**ning **bright**ly **in** the **night**)*

This sounds quite a normal way of speaking and happens to be in iambic pentameter, the most favoured of all meters and used invariably by many beginners when first starting to write poetry. Iambic pentameter is also found as a strict requirement in some forms of written poetry as, for example, in standard sonnets.

However, we need not concern ourselves with any of this at the moment, except to appreciate that a regular meter has imposed itself on the line of poetry. In the above example, both "shining" and "brightly" have retained their word accents, and so they sound right.

Discord

Let us now suppose that we had written the following line instead:

> The bright and silent stars shining at night
> *(The **bright** and **si**lent **stars** shi**ning** at **night**)*

This line has the same meter and says the same thing. Invariably, as in this example, the line stress will predominate, but in this case this results in a conflict between stress and accent when attempting to wedge the word "shining" into the line. We would never, normally, pronounce the word as shi-**ning**, and to do so jars upon the ear. The line no longer flows and quite simply this is not poetry.

If there are any lessons to be learnt about the art of writing poetry, then the fundamental one must surely be that poetry has to sound right. It may employ any number of clever constructions and may include all manner of descriptive words and phrases...but it has to sound like a normal way of speaking.

Poets aren't aliens, unable to comprehend the normal use of English in a clear way, and nor are their readers.

Compromise

Fortunately, there is a third alternative to the consideration of a dominant line stress, where a word may lose its accent to achieve poetical harmony. Here, a change in meter illustrates this effect:

> Stars shining brightly are silent as night
> *(**Stars** shining **bright**ly are **si**lent as **night**)*

As can be seen, "brightly" has retained its word accent, whereas "shining" has lost its accent in favour of the stress or meter of the line. Having done so, however, this is still of a quite natural consequence, and therefore sounds correct. One may argue that we would never speak quite like this, but poetry has always been endowed with a freedom of expression, the so-called "poetic licence". It is what makes a great poem memorable.

Pauses

Whilst we may look to find a regular meter in much of the poetry we read and write, there will always be occasions when a pause or hesitation is required, often indicated by the use of punctuation, and necessary sometimes to give added emphasis.

We will look at types of meter later, but for now we may see how this can vary in our simple example, and always be in harmony with the required word accents.

Stars: bright shining beacons in the silent night
*(**Stars**: **bright** shining **bea**cons **in** the **si**lent **night**)*

The pause between the stressed words of "stars" and "bright" gives added drama and pushes us forward to complete the line.

Punctuation

Before moving on, this is an appropriate time to mention the use of punctuation. Any writer must have an awareness of the importance of this established method by which small marks are used to indicate the way in which the sentences or lines of poetry are intended to be read. Brief pauses come with commas, longer pauses with semi-colons; and almost a complete halt with the colon: not quite but nearly, until we finally arrive at the aptly named full stop.

Sometimes a hyphen may achieve a slightly elongated pause - not to be confused with the in-between use of a dash. A similar effect may be achieved by an ellipsis... a series of dots (never more than three) that allow a continuation of the theme to follow. There's a need to understand the apostrophe too.

Do I need to explain the question mark? Certainly not!

We need only note how poetry that lacks punctuation shows a lack of understanding of its importance by the writer, and may well cause confusion in the reader as a result.

It may be appropriate to conclude this section with another example. The poem that follows illustrates the way in which words are selected so that their accents occur in harmony with the line stresses, despite several variations in meter.

Clearly the choice of words is necessary to convey meaning, as well the use of punctuation and other poetical considerations. Ultimately, the aim of the poem as a whole is to have a smooth flow, allowing us to think about what is being expressed.

KNOWING

It is not that the night is dark and cold,
or the stars that shine so clear and bright.

It is not that we see our love unfold
from poetry written in the night.

It is not that we stand beneath a sky
of silver dust, on a cloth of black –

or dare to dream, and not question why
the silence draws our memories back.

It is none of this, though we know it true
as the stars that shine through infinity...

it is knowing now of this time with you,
and the days and the nights we have still to see.

Use of Meter

Background

All poetry, with the possible exception of free verse, depends for part of its depth and appeal on the use of meter. Even free verse will be found to have a metric quality, although more akin to normal speech.

The meter does more than link the words together into a recognised melodic flow of lines. In much the same way as the choice of words may express varying degrees of emotion, so too may the choice of meter impart some particular quality to what is being said.

Getting Started

Meters come in all shapes and sizes and with a variety of names. Not that we need initially concern ourselves unduly with their names, as long as we have an appreciation of their effect.

Most people, when they begin writing poetry, will do so using an **iambic meter**....

The <u>**moon**</u> was <u>**clear**</u> and <u>**bright**</u> last <u>**night**</u>
ti-***TUM***, ti-***TUM***, ti-***TUM*** ti-***TUM***, .

As previously noted, the iambic meter often mirrors normal speech, which accounts for the frequency of its use. It is not always consciously chosen, as such, but is more often a default choice. This is no bad thing and if, for example, we pause to read any of Shakespeare's sonnets, we will find that these were written in this meter. In fact, all standard sonnets should be written in iambic pentameter, although some "modern" variation may occur from time to time.

Each portion of meter is said to be a "foot", so the example above is said to be a line with four feet. Later we will look at lines with any number of feet, and how they are used to best effect.

The poem that follows is an example of the use of iambic pentameter, which is to say that we can count five iambic feet for each line of the poem. It has a simple construction and reads in much the same way as we might normally express what we want to say. It is this natural feel that explains why the iambic meter is frequently used in poetry.

NIGHT MAGIC

How magical the bedroom was last night:
the stars that shone so clear…the moon so bright,
and touched by silver as we lay in bed.

And how I lay awake and could not sleep:
the hushed hours passing by, that seemed to keep
some gentle thoughts that I had found instead.

How magical it was; your hand in mine,
though you were lost to dreams that might combine
thoughts of the day with those of what may be.

Likewise my thoughts, as I lay calm and still;
the moon so bright, whereby it seemed to fill
the room with magic that I came to see…

and knew it to be true for you and me.

One thing we may notice about this poem is that the use of meter is not divided by the individual words, but flows on through them along the complete line.

For example:

How **mag** i **cal** the **bed** room **was** last **night**:
*ti-**TUM**, ti-**TUM**, ti-**TUM** ti-**TUM** ti-**TUM***

If we consider the word "magical" we see that it has three syllables, and in normal speech we would place emphasis on just the first syllable (**mag**-i-cal). However with the dominant line stress in iambic meter, we find ourselves placing an added stress on the third syllable. In doing so we do not alter the meaning of the word, nor does it jar on the ear. The iambic meter begins ahead of the word and simply flows on through it.

This poem is also chosen to illustrate how "rules" can be adapted to suit what we want to say. Each stanza has three lines with pairs of stanzas linked by their rhyme scheme. We will use the convention of letters to indicate matching rhymes, from which we have the following rhymes for the first four stanzas:

aab   ccb   dde   ffe

However an additional single line has been added to complete what was being said in the poem:

aab   ccb   dde   ffe   e

The poem could have stopped short of this line, but didn't. If this additional line had not been thought necessary, it would not be there... but it was and so it is. In all things rules must bend to suit the poem and not the poem to fit the rules, and that's what poetry is all about.

Moving Forward

Before starting to look at the many other types of meters available to us, we might like to ask ourselves how will we know which one to use for a poem? It's a good question, and one that doesn't have a simple answer.

Poets rarely have any preconceived notion of which meter they may use when they begin a poem. The inspiration of the poem itself will include some "feel" for whether the lines need to convey some fast, slow, abrupt, soft, mysterious... or whatever other emotional effect is required of the meter.

Most often the poem comes in a form or pace that seems "right", and the general inclination is to write this down as it is. Poems written this way will invariably have a natural flow and sound correct.

Sometimes, however, the poet may want to introduce some added emphasis to the poem, through the construction of a stanza with a defined meter. Again, this will probably have a natural feel to it, but this early choice of form may often bring an added quality.

Suppose, for example, we want to give the impression of speed – a sense of galloping along, then we would use an **anapaestic meter**:

> And the **thun**der of **hooves** as we **rode** on our **way**
> *ti-ti-**TUM** ti-ti-**TUM** ti-ti-**TUM** ti-ti-**TUM***

It will also be found that the iambic and anapaestic meters can be readily mixed together to give a variety of pace, although always with due regard to the requirements of word accent within the line stress, as has been previously considered.

Both meters have strong (masculine) endings and blend into a dynamic motion.

For example:

> He had **moved** as **fast** as he **thought** he **might**,
> *ti-ti-**TUM** ti-**TUM** ti-ti-**TUM** ti-**TUM***
>
> and had **paused** to **rest** through the **peace**ful **night**
> *ti-ti-**TUM** ti-**TUM** ti-ti-**TUM** ti-**TUM***

The poem that follows shows how the mixing of meters can add interest and drams to what is being said, so that the lines begin to sound more poetical, but in a natural way. The poem also uses metaphor to add depth to the meaning: it is not about swimming or indeed drowning as we quickly come to realise.

DROWNING MAN

He awoke from the depths, like a drowning soul
having risen up on the morning tide.
Up...slowly up...to the mournful grey
of another uninspiring day –
with a drifting awareness that sought to annul
what little ambition he tried to hide.

Yet risen there with him, the tattered shred
of a faint, fading dream, which had held him deep
in the dark, hidden depths of suspended gloom.
A slow, swirling current of hope in the room,
like wishes we seek and yet likewise dread,
from mysterious regions of darkness and sleep.

A grey, ebbing tide and a drawing in
of the nets, which we hope may still capture more
than our wearisome spirit might try to reach.
The returning of waves to a lonely beach –
a drowning man risen again to begin
his long swim to the dim and far-distant shore.

Review

We have already considered how meter may add a nuance of expression to the poem, to reflect and often endorse what is being said in words.

Both the **iambic meter** (*ti-**TUM***) and the **anapaestic meter** (*ti-ti-**TUM***) have strong (masculine) endings and blend well together. It is hardly surprising, therefore, to find examples of this in many well-known poems.

Occasionally the writing of a poem may come to be expressed in a way not normally found in everyday conversation, and may be deemed "poetical" in this sense. However, it should not sound as if we have stepped back a few centuries, either in terms of meter or use of language.

THOUGH WE ARE GROWN OLD

Though we are grown old
and are wise in the ways of the world –
though we know of the passing of days
and of history unfurled.
Though we stand with the knowledge of family
building upon
the lost generations once known,
which have come and have gone.
Though we look on achievements
and think ourselves grown to full height:
the time of our learning long past
and now faded from sight.

Yet we are but children
at times of bereavement and pain:
at times of farewell to the few
who took time to explain
what they knew about life,
with the knowledge they shared and discussed.
A time we had nothing to give in return,
but our trust
and our love...and a faith in their words
and a truth, which survives
from knowing how they would remain
as a part of our lives.

Though we are grown old,
yet as children we bid them farewell.
Our album of childhood lies open
where memories dwell –
with images faded, yet memories bright as before,
that the love and the sorrow...
the laughter and pain remain raw.
This our final farewell, and yet never to thoughts,
which will hold
us as children forever,
although we must likewise grow old.

Softer Meters

Softer meters with (feminine) unstressed word endings are able to provide a more gentle feel to the poem, and this we find with the **trochaic meter (*TUM-ti*)**

By way of example, consider the following:

<u>Let</u> us <u>speak</u> of <u>oth</u>er <u>matt</u>ers
***TUM**-ti **TUM**-ti **TUM**-ti **TUM**-ti*

Again, we should note the agreement between word accent and line stress for "<u>oth</u>er" and "<u>matt</u>ers" as well as the overall softness of the line

A famous and lengthy poem written in trochaic tetrameter (4 feet) is "The Song of Hiawatha" written in 1855 by Henry Wadsworth Longfellow (1770 - 1850). The poem is said to be based on American Indian legends and folk stories, but what is immediately apparent is the way in which the meter "echoes" a typical drumbeat rhythm.

"<u>By</u> the <u>shores</u> of <u>Git</u>che <u>Gu</u>mee..."
***TUM**-ti **TUM**-ti **TUM**-ti **TUM**-ti*

Curiously, the poem was not well received by critics at the time with some scathing reviews, although it quickly found popularity amongst the many readers who purchased copies of the book. It is always as well to remember when forming an opinion that a poem may mean different things to different people.

In any event, the attitude adopted by Longfellow was one of having produced a romantic epic literary work with which he was well pleased. Again, we should write for ourselves, and if others find something worthy in what we do, then this is an added bonus.

A pastiche of this poem, written with the same distinctive meter, is included later in the poem **"Brighton Days"**(page 89).

Moving On

Another gentle meter is the **dactylic meter** (***TUM**-ti-ty*)

> **This** is the **rea**son why **we** had been **whis**pering
> ***TUM**-ti-ty **TUM**-ti-ty **TUM**-ti-ty **TUM**-ti-ty*

> **BEACONS OF HAPPINESS**
>
> *Softly and slowly the day now declining,*
> *fading in puddles of orange and gold.*
> *Lingering sunset: the clouds gilded lining*
> *drifting as onward the hour grows old.*
>
> *Gathering shadows of delicate twilight,*
> *hung like a curtain of gossamer grace.*
> *Purple horizon and faint glint of starlight*
> *lost in the dark cosmic velvet of space.*
>
> *Likewise our memories, lingering lightly:*
> *yesterday's grey in the distance of days.*
> *Beacons of happiness gleaming as brightly -*
> *guiding our path along wandering ways.*

Maintaining the Mood

It is hardly surprising to discover that the trochaic and dactylic meters can be readily mixed together, although frequently this is done more for atmospheric effect rather than a change of pace.
(See also later notes on the Sapphic stanza - page 120).
For example:

> **Deep** in the **for**est, **phan**toms had **gath**ered
> ***TUM**-ti-ty **TUM**-ti **TUM**-ti-ty **TUM**-ti*
>
> **si**lently... **si**lently **drift**ing in **shad**ows
> ***TUM**-ti-ty, **TUM**-ti-ty, **TUM**-ti-ty, **TUM**-ti)*

The example that follows has stanzas which are predominantly in the dactylic meter, intended to provide a "soft" feel to what is a romantic poem.

LADY... FAIR LADY

Lady... fair lady of lilac and blue
in a dress of soft lace, and a beauty so true.
Your warm hand in mine, as we dance for a while -
lost in the charm of your wonderful smile,
and ever and always my true love for you.

Lady...fair lady, these moments we share:
the silver of moonlight... the gold in your hair.
The soft music playing this warm summer's eve
when, briefly, I pause and can hardly believe
this magic with you and the love that we share.

And ever and always the depth in your eyes
that mirror the infinite blue of the skies.
Your soft lips, so red, kissing troubles away
at times when we face sombre clouds, dark and grey...
and always our love, beyond any disguise.

Lady... fair lady, these words are but few
that tell of my love and affection for you.
A bright inspiration, whereby I may place
such words as speak always of our warm embrace,
and of love... my fair lady in lilac and blue.

An easy combination of trochaic and dactylic meters is also seen in the following poem, which is emphasised slightly by an unusual rhyme scheme of irregularly paired stanzas

abbc, addc, efe, gfg, hjjk, hllk

We will look at various rhyme patterns later.

A SIMPLE VERSE

This will be a simple verse,
for there are no magic words –
just the few that you have heard
many times before.

This, the pageant we rehearse:
this the love that has grown old
and a story long-since told.
Truth forever sure.

This, the simple verse I write:
this the candle flame of love,
burning brightly in the night.

These few words and nothing more,
with the honesty of love
soft as waves upon the shore.

These, the passing days we share.
These, my words in simple rhyme
but a token of our time...
bright with happy themes.

Simple as the gift of prayer –
love from magic moments found.
Bright with treasured moments, bound
in a book of dreams.

Other meters

Needless to say there exist a great many more than just the four meters we have considered so far - in fact the ancient Greeks knew of more than thirty distinct forms! Many of these are not used in English poetry, although a summary of this impressive variety is provided (for interest only) on page 265.

Greek plays and recited poetry at that time required the use of specific meters according to various subjects (ancient gods and such) and a formality in the way these were to be addressed and presented. A reminder, perhaps, that poetry owes its origins to performance, as well as to the written word.

Thankfully, modern English poetry has escaped the confines of such strict rules and a mastery of the four meters we have seen – namely the iambic, anapaestic, trochaic and dactylic - will satisfy the majority of poems we wish to write.

There are, however, a few other meters and use of metric variation, which we should consider, since they do occur from time to time, and can be used to startling effect!

The Monosyllabic Pause

A pause might hardly be considered to be a type of meter, although clearly it does affect the flow of words, and by creating a momentary halt in a line of poetry this can have a very dramatic effect. This will often add weight to what has immediately preceded it, whilst focusing attention on what is to follow.

Since the mixing of meters can create varying emphases at irregular intervals, and may in themselves add lesser pauses, the question arises as to how we might be able to come to a sudden halt, before setting off once more? This can only be readily achieved by having one stressed syllable followed immediately by another – the monosyllable.

This is probably best shown by example, such as the start of "Sea Fever" by John Edward Masefield (1878 - 1967)

*"I **must** go **down** to the **sea** a**gain**,*
*to the **lone**ly **sea** and the **sky**,*
*And **all** I **ask** is a **tall ship** and a **star** to **steer** her **by**;"*

The mixed iambic (*ti-**TUM***) and anapaestic (*ti-ti-**TUM***) meters are suddenly halted by the "**tall ship**" *(**TUM**-**TUM**)* before we move forward again.

We could well think of other examples ourselves.
For example:

> "I will **pause** for a **while; pause** and move **on**
> with a **mo**ment of **si**lence, **come** and **gone**"

Correct punctuation shows the use of a semi-colon to indicate a slight pause between the two stressed syllables, although with the choice of words we could hardly not hesitate anyway.

Amphibrachic Meter

But for the existence of the limerick, it is doubtful whether we might ever come to know and appreciate the amphibrachic meter quite as well as we do. This ancient Greek meter has a stressed middle of three syllables, thus (*ti-**TUM**-ty*)

> "There **was** a young **la**dy from **Lon**don...
> *ti-**TUM**-ty, ti-**TUM**-ty, ti-**TUM**-ty*

In the limerick, the third meter endings are often carried over into the start of the next line, but the overall effect remains the same:

> *There was a young fellow named Sid,*
> *who was warned of car defects well hid.*
> *"Don't forget, check your brakes,*
> *you could die from mistakes" –*
> *but he did and he didn't and did.*

It would be foolish to suppose that this meter cannot be used in a more serious manner.

For example:

DEPARTURE

*Our friend in the hospital lay,
gravely ill and just fading away.
The doctors were sure
of a week... maybe more:
but he left us the very next day.*

LIMERICK RHYME

*The limerick works as a rhyme
since the meter is truly sublime.
The words may be crude
with rude meanings quite lewd -
and yet funny, for most of the time*

The amphibrachic meter itself provides a sense of movement, with hardly any opportunity for a brief rest. For this reason, it will also be found as a "linking" meter in poems of mixed meter, as shown by the poem that follows.

FIRST OF THE FEW

I am the first – the first of the few.
Others may follow and do what I do,
but I am the first
and the best and the worst of the few.

I am the leader – the one pioneer.
Where I go, none has been -
there are none venture near.
For I am the first of the few that will be –
and the few that will follow
must all follow me.

I am the adventurer venturing on...
seeking to go where none other has gone.
The brave and the bold and the wild and the free
will learn of my journey,
and then follow me.

For I am the first and the first of the few.
Let legends record all the things that I do:
the places I go
and the things that I see.
My destiny waits upon things yet to be.

History, mystery, fable and fact...
the wonder of magic: the truth of each act.
The deeds that are done and of deeds still to do –
all woven in time, in a tapestry true
to the chosen adventure...
the brave and the new.
For I am the first
and the first of the few.

Paeon (Paean)

Having mentioned the variety of Greek meters, it is with the paeon that we begin to venture a little way into this slightly foreign territory. From the more popular metric divisions of two and three syllables, we now undertake a consideration of meters with four syllables.

On the one hand, this will greatly test our agreement between word accent and line stress (which may well account for the fact that it is seldom used) although there is a degree of "flexibility" offered, in as much as the stressed syllable may fall anywhere amongst the four.

These are known appropriately enough as the 1st, 2nd, 3rd & 4th paeon

TUM-ti-ti-ty Ti-*TUM*-ti-ty Ti-ti-*TUM*-ty Ti-ti-ti-*TUM*

We have still to decide on which of the four options best suits what we want to write, and accept that we are then committed to this same arrangement throughout the whole poem. There is no "mix and match" possible, since this would quickly become akin to free verse, with no discernible pattern to the flow of words.

It is possibly for this reason, and the likelihood of conflict between word accents and line stresses that the paeon meter is not often to be found in poems. One notable exception, perhaps, is the example shown in "Kubla Khan" by Samuel Taylor Coleridge (1772 - 1834), which begins:

"In **Xan**adu did **Ku**bla Khan a **state**ly pleasure-**dome** decree:"
ti-*TUM*-ti-ty   ti-*TUM*-ti-ty   ti-*TUM*-ti-ty   ti-*TUM*-ti-ty

Poems written using this meter tend to "run away" very quickly, and conflicts with word accent do require special attention. The final effect, however, is often well worth the added perspiration!

The paeon may also be carefully mixed with other masculine meters, such as the iambic and anapaestic.

For example:

"It's **been** a while since **I** sat down and **tried** to write a **rhyme**"
*ti-**TUM**-ti-ty   ti-**TUM**-ti-ty   ti-**TUM**-ti-ty   ti-**TUM***

This first line is taken from the poem that follows, written using the paeon meter to illustrate also how long the lines can become, even when (as in this case) they have only four feet. For this reason, the lines are often divided into two parts, as the poem shows:

COMING OF THE RAIN

*It's been a while since I sat down
and tried to write a rhyme –
the days just passed so quickly
that I had not found the time.
The ideas came and went –
although I hoped they'd come again,
between the days of sunshine
and the coming of the rain.*

*The sunny days of May are here
and there is much to do,
and each bright new good morning
brings contentment, this is true.
Between what's done today
or what tomorrow may explain,
with the coming of a rainbow
should I chance to see the rain.*

*Now those who know of songs
will know of one that fills my head –
though as to how or why
I cannot reason now instead.
It seems I woke this morning
with the words etched on my brain –
how Dylan sheltered from the storm
and I looked for the rain.*

It's been so long...too long it seems,
since pen-strokes filled the page,
and caged within a lack of inspiration for an age.
From something new and something true –
these thoughts that still remain,
throughout the changing seasons
of the sun and wind and rain.

So now I sit awhile
and let my thoughts just wander free –
unsure where they may take me
but with time enough to see.
Content enough to sit and write
and never once complain,
how words may then come flooding
like a sudden fall of rain.

And this I hope, beyond the time
that this rhyme comes to show,
of many more to follow –
though of this I may not know.
The sudden storm of passion
and the prize I hope to gain,
that comes from days of sunshine
and the coming of the rain.

In the example above and the one that follows, it can be seen that the 2nd paeon meter (*ti-**TUM**-ti-ty*) if kept constant throughout would leave us with a double "soft" (unstressed) ending to each line.

This would appear as if the words were fading away, which might work for some particular theme, although normally it would be better to have a stressed (masculine) ending.

A truncated paean meter (*ti-**TUM***) - which we recognise immediately as our ubiquitous iambic meter, is therefore an ideal choice.

THE TURNING OF THE SEASONS

The turning of the seasons
brings the years that come and go -
from days of summer sunshine
to the chill of winter's snow.
From promises of springtime
to the autumn harvest won –
the turning of the seasons
and another year begun.

The passing of the hours
brings the days we come to share,
that leave us with bright memories
of which we are aware.
And from the many moments
there may linger then the few
that we will long remember,
and will never fade from view.

And so it is we now recall a time of long ago –
a time of love and promises
that we have come to know.
This happy anniversary,
which serves to illustrate
the turning of the seasons,
and the love we celebrate.

A Summary So Far...

The poem that follows is intended to demonstrate the effects of the different meters we have considered so far. In all cases, we have seen how meter is used to provide a steady flow of words, which can enhance the meaning of the words themselves by means of pace and emphasis. Certain meters can be used to give a swift movement and can quickly gallop away with us, whilst others will deliberately slow down what we wish to say, and introduce a soft, even slightly mystical quality to our words.

METRIC WIT

There are many forms of meter,
which may serve the modern writer.
Here, trochaic feet skip neater
for a pace made light and brighter.

Yet to quicken the pace with a thundering air,
it is then anapaestic is best!
With a feeling for movement made plainly aware,
it will gallop ahead of the rest.

And yet, more popular it seems,
iambic meter, sure and strong,
is guaranteed to capture dreams
and move the poetry along.

Finally dactylic meter comes lumbering —
eager for service, with nimble agility.
Sure as a drum-beat to waken thoughts slumbering:
happy to demonstrate this capability.

Whilst added to meters and carefully written
the bold amphibrachic we must also mention.
Though clearly of limericks frequently smitten,
this meter may often escape your attention.

Continually challenging, the paeon meter hurriedly
comes galloping across the page...
accelerating worriedly.
An uncontrolled experience:
alarming in its consequence,
yet magical the poetry
that comes with such exuberance.

And to end with a brief monosyllabic pause.
Note the effect: note too the cause.

The mixing of meters (as we will later see) is also extremely effective in introducing variation and interest, in much the same way as someone talking might place emphasis and pauses on what they are saying (see logaoedic poem - page 205). By comparison, a constant dull droning on can be very boring and soporific, and the aim is never that our poetry should send the reader to sleep!

We have already seen how poetry should generally emulate normal speech, and avoid any affected means of archaic expression. As with all rules, however, there is always an exception, and we will soon consider one unique form known as "sprung verse" (see page 52). A reminder for now, however, of our earlier observation that in poetry it is always okay to break the rules where necessary to achieve what we want to say.

Less Common Meters

We have already considered the more popular and some less frequent meters we might use. We know also that relatively few of the numerous forms of meter known to the ancient Greeks have found their way into modern English poetry (see page 265).

However, there remains three meters whose use in English poetry is extremely rare. Although they are seldom mentioned in many books on the subject, the very fact that they exist and can be used to unusual advantage surely warrants a brief consideration.

Anacrusis

The anacrusis is a non-stressed word or syllable at the start of a line, which does not contribute to the meter and acts simply as a "link" to follow forward on the flow of words from one line to the next. For example, the word "will" in the following...

> *The anacrusis in iambic verse*
> *will become a passing link and nothing worse.*

Spondee

The spondee has two stressed syllables, which using our convention becomes (***TUM -TUM***)

We might think of a two-syllable words that would have this natural emphasis, such as "midnight" although the placing of two stressed syllables in a line of poetry does present a challenge. For example "stopwatch" in the following...

Give the stopwatch to the captain
TUM -ti **TUM-TUM Tum**-ti **Tum**-ti

The use of the spondee, much like to monosyllabic pause, creates hesitation in the line, and whilst this may be used for effect, it may sometimes sound slightly disjointed and removed from normal speech. In as much as the normal aim of poetry is to create a flow of words, with the use of various meters to create rhythm and pace, it is hardly surprising that examples of the spondee are quite unusual.

Pyrrhic

The pyrrhic has two unstressed syllables (ti-ti), where a two-syllable word example might be used as a link. For example:

Coming like a ghost at twilight
Tum-ti ti-ti **Tum**-ty **TUM**-ty
iambi pyrrhic iambic iambic

Sprung Verse

We might hardly conclude any consideration of types of meter without a mention made of Gerard Manley Hopkins (1844 - 1889), and his unique use of what he described as "sprung verse". This flies in the face of our previous statement that poetry should flow and sound like normal speech, but does so in a quite distinct and highly disciplined way.

Consider then his poem "As Kingfishers Catch fire" where he has the lines

> *"Stones ring; like each tuckèd string tells, each hung bell's*
> *Bow swung finds tongue to fling out broad its name;"*

His use of language provides something of a struggle in itself, but this is further complicated by an analysis of the mixed meters being used, where emphasis on the words is as shown below.

> "Stones **ring**; like each **tuck**-ed **string tells**, each hung bell's
> **Bow swung** finds **tongue** to fling out **broad** its **name**;"

Anyone wishing to emulate this form of staccato meter will quickly discover how extremely convoluted it can be, particularly if mixed liberally with the use of assonance and irregular internal rhyme, for which Gerard Manly Hopkins was also noted.

That said, his descriptive imagery is quite excellent, with use of metaphor and several layers of meaning, often difficult to follow, although any struggle to come to terms with what is being said is well worth the effort. It is doubtful indeed that we might wish to emulate this style, although an example in the form of a sonnet is shown in the poem "**Everlong**" (see page 157).

Irregular Meter

All poetry should have a sense of flow, giving a cohesion to the words. This is often achieved through the use of an appropriate meter, and any predilection towards the lesser constraints offered by free verse cannot entirely ignore the need for a natural cadence in the use of words. Basically it has to sound like normal speech, with a natural rhythm.

The example that follows includes the deliberate use of an irregular and staccato meter, which is intended to capture something of the noise and confusion experienced whilst visiting New York, with all of the traffic and crowded places typical of a major city.

The line lengths are long, in order to provide the sensation of "rushing along" with the desired hesitancy at occasional intervals, much as one might tend to pause whilst sight-seeing to look at something in a shop window. In this case it was a pair of brightly coloured shoes.

NEW YORK – NEW SHOES

In New York this bright, noisy, loud, ever-busy new day,
we arrive at the pier on the ferry from New Jersey shore.
Between canyons of concrete and steel,
as we stroll on our way,
with time enough now just to wander
and slowly explore.

Through Soho and Chelsea,
where bookshops and art shops are found.
Past Italian restaurants and bright,
crowded cafés we go –
and parks with tall fountains...
whilst ever around us the sound
of the yellow-cab traffic and rush of New York city flow.

And then in a sporting shop window, we happen to see
many things we might like,
so I enter and finally choose
a souvenir gift, which I know to be typically me:
my red, blue, green, yellow and purple,
black, orange new shoes.

There are gifts we will buy on our holiday,
still left to find:
bright colourful tokens to purchase
and take on our way.
But of all we may have,
my new shoes will be there to remind
of our time in New York on a busy and bright, noisy day.

A Flexible Approach

Conventionally, most rhyming poetry will be of a recognised construction. We will come to look at this relationship as found in several traditional forms later, but can accept for now that there is often a recognised arrangement between rhyme and meter.

However, it should it be assumed that rhyming poetry will always necessarily have a regular meter or length of lines. For example:

IF IT COMES TO BE

*If it comes to be
that I forget the date...the day...the year.
If things become unclear
and slip away from me.*

*If places blur, and faces too
are smiling strangers in my day,
with memories that drift away
of those I knew.*

*If yesterdays become unclear
like faded photo's on a shelf.
If I no longer know myself,
nor smile...nor speak...nor shed a tear.*

*Know only this, how love must dwell
within the shell of hidden sight,
in thoughts caught up in nets of light
we once knew well.*

*And know of what was true and free
of love and life that souls may share
must linger there,
in this pale ghost you see in me:
precious still, though unaware
if it comes to be*

The previous poem has a simple rhyme form (abba), which is known as an envelope stanza, but is disguised slightly by both an irregular meter and length of lines, as shown in.

        *If it **comes** to **be***   *(ti-ti-**TUM**, ti-**TUM**)*

        *that I forg**et** the **date**...the **day**...the **year**.*
        *(ti-ti-ti-**TUM**, ti-**TUM**, ti-**TUM**, ti-**TUM**)*

        *If **things** become un**clear***   *(ti-**TUM**, ti-ti-ti-**TUM**)*
        *and **slip** a**way** from **me**.*   *(ti-**TUM**, ti-**TUM**, ti-**TUM**)*

Natural Rhythm

We know that free verse avoids any form of rhyme or regular meter, and is reliant on a natural rhythm and form of expression. The flow of words along a line will include a more casual use of stress to accentuate what is being said, together with a mixing of meters.

For example:

        Waves do not **ent**er **here**: **ev**en when the **tide** is **low**
        TUM ti-ti-**TUM** ti-**TUM**: **TUM**-ti ti-ti-**TUM** ti-**TUM**

This may allow for a descriptive use of language and is usually achieved through a succinct number of words.

The ability to discard the use of a strict or uniform meter also allows for interpretation by the reader with regards to when and where pauses may be taken to enhance the meaning...to linger for a while before moving on.

This is ideal for performance poetry and can imbue the poem with added meaning.

The following poem shows how this may be achieved.

GREEN SANCTUARY

Waves do not enter here: even when the tide is low,
the cavern mouth remains submerged and hidden,
swallowing the flood of water.

Outside, beyond a wall of rock, the waves explode...
collapse into a lathered scum.
Wisps of white spume drenching the rock face:
the bitter tang of salt stinging the air.

Yet hushed within this hollow dome of stone,
a gentle rise and fall of mirror surface
is all that marks the sea's returning.

A bosom of water breathing softly
in harmony with the tide's continued ebb and flow.

And entering this peaceful realm, diffused sunlight
glows through a fathom's depth of misty brine:
an opaque screen of green and clouded water

where a thousand emerald gems sparkle and gleam,
reflected from the particles of sand
and stirred debris of broken shells.

And deeper yet...
where seaweed shredded into transparent ribbons,
sways in harmony
with the sea's soft melancholy tune.

Sudden fish!
Darting like silver phantoms,
as if aware of secrets
whispered by leviathans of the distant ocean.

Here in this sanctuary:
this vaulted cathedral of sea and rock.
This place of quiet calm where waves may not enter
nor sea erode the solitude of time.

We might compare the previous use of free verse to describe a seascape with the following rhyming poem, where the pattern has been deliberately mixed to make the rhyme less obvious and intrusive.

FOWEY HARBOUR

A drizzle, gentle as a sigh,
sifts slowly through the silent trees
whilst shrouded clouds, of winter grey,
from far across the distant shore
are ushered gently overhead,
like weary mourners of the day.
A sombre chill descends once more
across the harbour, soon to spread
in veils of mist sent drifting by
like vague, uncertain memories.

Safe in the harbour, tethered boats
ride on the swell of rising tide,
as small waves slap drenched wooden hulls
with ghostly, echoed slow applause
for their frail mastery of the sea.
And overhead, the white-winged gulls
float in a thin, chill-morning gauze
of hazy sky…aimless and free,
to scream in harsh, discordant notes
as onward through their realm they glide.

Bright, broken mirrors catch the dawn
upon the surface of the sea,
where deep and silent, dark below
the waters swirl in sudden thrust
of rippling, silver-muscled flight.
The glint and gleam in eerie glow,
where twisting fins sense and adjust
to hidden currents…twist and fight:
and seeking somewhere calm to spawn
a brine-bold warrior hunts the sea.

Final Words

It is not always necessary to know the name of whatever meter is being used, but it is important to recognise that it is there. In later notes we will come to look at the division of lines according to use of meter and lengths in terms of the number of feet. For example, the classical sonnet will have fourteen lines in a pre-determined rhyme scheme, and will be written in iambic pentameter. Modern sonnets may "bend" these rules slightly.

To conclude our look at the many types of meter, it is as well to remind ourselves that a choice is there to enhance the poem...not complicate it. Many traditional forms of poetry use fairly simple meters, such as the villanelle written in iambic tetrameters (4 feet).

SUMMER SKIES

Whenever I see summer skies
of endless, deep and perfect blue,
I think about your smiling eyes.

I think of you, and realise
how sad I am away from you –
whenever I see summer skies.

And should the day seek grey disguise,
my memory remains as true.
I think about your smiling eyes

of perfect blue, that symbolise
the days we shared and love we knew –
whenever I see summer skies.

Though seasons change, and I grow wise
to dreams of dim and distant view,
I think about your smiling eyes...

as if my thoughts might prophesise
a time of change: yet certain too,
whenever I see summer skies
I think about your smiling eyes.

Use of Rhyme

Once Upon a Time...

Once upon a time, the use of rhyme combined with a good steady meter served well as an aid in remembering some epic saga, when such tales predated literacy and relied on oral recitals. Poetry, at this time, spoke of recent deeds, battles won, great kings and heroes remembered.

Ballads sung by travelling minstrels were often of such heroic tales - poetry set to music - and might be readily changed to suit local circumstances. Some recent event or the name of a new king would enhance the reception that such ballads might expect to receive.

The traditional use of rhyme continued beyond a time when poetry was written down and people were able to read it for themselves. It added a musical quality to the use of words... an added charm. Indeed it was almost the very use of rhyme that for many centuries defined what a poem was expected to be. It was not until the introduction of "vers libre" during the late 19th century by poets such as Arthur Rimbaud (1854-1891) that a form of non-rhyming lines was finally to be considered as poetry.

With free verse came an opportunity to break away from tradition, and this has continued, allowing many modern poets to liberate themselves of this constraint. Many feel that they are best able to express themselves without the use of rhyme, whilst others still prefer the poetical benefits that rhyme can bring.

A Cautious Start

One of the major pitfalls encountered when using rhyme is not in the search for a word of the same sound – the English language abounds with such words. No... the problem (if such) is in finding a word that not only sounds right, but also makes sense and adds to the flow of what is being expressed.

There is also the temptation of inversion to consider, where the normal construction of a sentence is changed in order to finish with a desired rhyme.

> *"The normal construction of grammar is changed by some,*
> *so that rhyme at the end of a selected line will come."*

Another major criticism of rhyme is in its misuse, when the poet may settle upon any word of the desired phonetic sound, irrespective of the fact that it doesn't form part of what is being expressed.

> *"I went for a walk, and I heard the trees talk."*

Now leaves may (poetically) seem to whisper in the breeze but trees do not talk, and to suggest this begins to make nonsense of the whole thing.

Another consideration when using rhyme is the "sledge-hammer" effect that can also arise from an ill-considered word at the end of each line. The last thing needed is to hit the reader with a sudden blow, which may prevent a smooth onward flow. The same is true for the use of internal rhyme, which occurs mid-way along a line, and must also avoid any jarring effect.

> *"I went to see the tall oak tree - it was as tall as tall could be."*

This is possibly fine for children's verse, where there is a deliberate emphasis on the rhyme, but from our earlier considerations, this is verse rather than poetry.

A final word of caution comes from the use of obvious rhymes. There will always be a "breeze" in the "trees" but it has been said so many times and has lost its originality. Is there, perhaps, a less obvious rhyme that needs to be found?

Types of Rhyme

We all know what rhyme is...or do we? In actual fact, rhyme is never quite as simple as we might think and comes in all manner of guises, which can vary from the obvious to the more subtle.

Masculine and Feminine Rhymes

From our previous look meters we know some (such as iambic and anapaestic) to be strong and masculine. They are bold and invariably make a statement, which probably explains their preferred use in much rhyming poetry, giving a decisive finish to the lines.

However, we know also of the softer meters (trochaic and dactylic) that have un-accentuated endings, such as "gently" or "tenderly". Feminine endings may slow the movement of a poem but can create mood and atmosphere. In this way, the choice of meter can start to influence rhyme, as shown by the choice of a paeon meter (**TUM**-ti-ti-ty) in the following example:

DEEDS DONE WELL

Much there was of deeds and dreaming:
much I will not do again.
Bright ambitions, sharp and gleaming,
tarnished by the years, and seeming
set aside, where they have lain.

Much once known from ancient history –
quests, like branches, grown and planned.
Many journeys made from this tree,
shrouded now in mists and mystery
of a vast, forgotten land.

Many moments made from measures
gathered up a thousand-fold.
Noble deeds and former pleasures:
golden gifts and bolder treasures
here in memories I hold.

Deeds done well – yet abdicating
realms of wonder I once knew.
Former glories then abating –
and of new adventures waiting,
left for others now to do.

True Rhyme

True rhyme is based purely on the phonetic sounds of words, irrespective of spelling. For example, "blew, true, who" are true rhymes, though clearly different in their spelling. True rhyme is, in fact, what many of us might consider to be the only form of rhyme, although there are other types.

A word of caution too when using true rhyme, which comes with a need to take account of dialect and variations in the way that words are said. In the north of England, for example, "mast" would be seen to rhyme with "gassed" whereas in the south "mast" would have an "arst" sound.

So-called "Queen's English" may hold good in most cases, but if the poem is set in a particular place or ethnic group, then it is as well to reflect any local dialect and the way that words are enunciated. This may also entail having to "play" with the spelling of words, to indicate the way in which they are to be pronounced.

As shown by the following example, poetry is often presented as a performance art in the way it is read. There are many examples by famous poets where, to ensure the correct dialect pronunciation of words, the poet is seen to write in a phonetical way to indicate the way that the words should sound.

For example, Robert Burns (1759 - 1796) in his poem *"To A Louse, On Seeing One on a Lady's Bonnet at Church"*.

> *"O wad some Pow'r the giftie gie us*
> *To see oursels as ithers see us!"*

> And would some Power the small gift give us
> To see ourselves as others see us!

Clearly a somewhat curious title and (presumably) an unusual source of inspiration too!

The poem that follows is also based on an actual incident as described.

MING KUNG CHEN

*Ming Kung Chen work foo west-a-want
wi chinee food deriv-a-lees.
Go many prace all velly klik
though Ingrish he no speak wi ease.*

*So rive wi chinee take-away
an gerrin rif to uppa froor...
But rif then stop! All velly dark
an rif no wanna star no more.*

*A rif no go a-down or up.
He showl ow loud all onis own
an pressa burrons...showl again,
ba no-wan risen. He arone.*

*Foo hole week-en he twap in rif.
He riv on noodle take-away.
Then fown on Too-day, velly ill,
though have no Ingrish words to say.*

*Police a-come an risen good.
No unner-standee wa he say
so wait... burra big boss-man come
an evry-fin a-soon okay.*

*He be much berrer velly klik —
go bakka work an happy there.
Ba forra new deriv-a-lees
he no use rif, ba walk up stair.*

Spelling Rhyme

Spelling rhyme is often seen in slightly archaic poetry, where in some instances the pronunciation of words may have differed from modern usage.

For example, at the time of Geoffrey Chaucer (1343 - 1400) "houres and youres" were both pronounced with an "oo-er" sound. The modern words of "hours and yours", whilst retaining a similar change in spelling have resulted in quite different pronunciations. An illustration of the way in which language, as a living thing, continues to evolve over a period of time.

Whilst spelling rhyme includes words that clearly look the same, they may often sound quite different. For example "love and move" or "foot and root"

Using true (phonetic) rhyme we would pair "foot with put" and "root with chute".

> *IN SEARCH OF RHYME*
>
> *Through many words and meanings*
> *we must diligently plough*
> *in search of rhyme...*
> *only to find the way is sometimes tough.*
>
> *For spelling may not lend a clue*
> *and can confuse...although*
> *we start to feel, perhaps,*
> *that we are trapped within a trough.*
>
> *And yet, determined for a while,*
> *we search the pages through,*
> *until we recognise a time*
> *when we have had enough.*

Para-rhyme or Consonant Rhyme

The para-rhyme is a term coined originally by Edmund Charles Blunden (1896 - 1974) to describe a form of "near rhyme" where consonants in two words are the same but vowels vary. The use of consonant rhyme, therefore, is a fairly new deliberate use of language, and can be applied to great effect.

For example "fit, fat, feet" are consonant rhymes, as in the following jogger's mantra:

Fast flying feet,
will fight the fat
and keep us fit.

Vowel Rhyme

It is hardly surprising to discover that we can do the same thing with vowels, usually with a linking consonant. For example "feet, feed, feel".

PROSODY

It is not death that comes with a sigh,
for death is silent, and always so.
No-matter what others choose to say
or, of a fancy, chance to see,
it is not death that comes with a sigh.

Yet the poet's voice will never die,
whose thoughts live on in prosody.
Though all must keep the appointment due,
as night must surely follow day –
yet the poet's voice will never die.

Application of Rhyme

The application of rhyme is usually dictated by the construction of the poem. For example, in four-line stanzas, and using letters to denote matching rhymes, then a common rhyme scheme will usually follow the format:

abab

This can be modified to provide many variations, such as:

abba, abba (envelope stanzaas) or couplets **aabb**.

Things start to get interesting if we match rhymes in consecutive stanzas, so that we start to achieve interlocked patterns such as:

aaba, bbcb, etc.

We will look at the construction of stanzas and forms of poetry in more detail at a later time, but for the moment it is as well to appreciate that any variation in the occurrence of rhyme is quite acceptable, and may often serve to enhance the poem.

Random Rhyme

Random rhyme is used to describe the application of rhyme in no discernible pattern, and frequently allows this to occur whenever and wherever may seem convenient. It may be irregular or spasmodic, but clearly serves also to ensure the avoidance of any obvious or anticipated rhyme, which can be a good thing.

A modern form of the sonnet (known as the Quatorzain) uses this form of irregular rhyme (see page 162).

When taken a step further, we may see this sense of freedom beginning to venture into the realms of free verse, with an occasional disregard of rhyme for one of more lines. Within this mêlée it will frequently pass un-noticed, whilst occasional rhymes appear to "chime" at odd intervals.

RESOLUTION

Just another night
at the turning of the year
with stars that pierce a cloudless sky
and the pale moon like a silent ghost
comes sliding by.

Wine and celebration –
fling wide the window,
pull in resolution from the chill night air.
It lingers there... somewhere

where the same dark shadows hide
our distant failures from last year
to let them fade, un-noticed:
disappear.

The same bright laughter now –
falls like an echo of our yesterday
with memories we will no longer treasure or deny:
a letting go that sees them slip away.

Come...come let us not dwell now
upon such solemn thoughts
when all is bright and new:
the brighter view untarnished yet
by sorrow or regret.

Let self-forgiveness fall like snow:
cover what we would not see.
Welcome the new, unwritten year.
The prospect clear...
a clean, white page
to set a new beginning free.

Positioning of Rhyme

We have mentioned the way in which an internal rhyme may occur mid-way along a line. Where this mid-rhyme is paired with a word at the end of that line it is sometimes known as Leonine verse, named after a 13th-centry Italian poet called Leo, who much-favoured this form of writing.

CODICIL

Many words have we spoken
from past thoughts awoken, and promises made
through the unbroken, long years together.
With dreams come and gone,
as a token of our time displayed –
which still tethers and binds us as one.

Many old secrets shared
from a time having dared to do much in the name.
of a cared-for awareness and youthfulness
long...long ago.
Young love that flared brightly and came
with a truthfulness...finding it so.

For this same love dwells still.
in desires we fulfil with a consummate ease,
and a codicil found in the autumn
of our gentle days.
The faint echo and thrill of old memories
caught in a gathering haze.

In other applications of internal rhyme, it may be found that mid-rhymes are paired with end of line words on other lines. This interplay or cross-rhyme between internal and end-line rhymes can be as varied as the rhymes themselves.

Softened Rhyme

Another way of softening the effects of rhyme is to arrange lines and stanzas so that natural breaks occur at intervals other than at the end of the lines. If the poem is then written in such a way as to reflect these divisions into normal speech, the rhymes appear more random and less noticeable.

DECEMBER DAYS

Cattle in the frosty field pause and stare
and do not yield their careful gaze as we pass by.
Content to watch with steady eye
our passing down the winding lane,
that sees us come and go again.

Distant in the view displayed
where now the blanched white pastures fade
into a morning mist that drifts through distant trees,
and later lifts revealing a chill-sparkle there,
where sunlight glows through morning air.

Cattle in the frosty field pause and stare...
their movement stilled, as if aware of frozen grass
they cannot graze...yet watch us pass,
content to wait for winter's sun.

December days, that slowly run
with silver frost and morning mist...
here kissed by silent hours this tryst.

Line-Start Rhymes

Sometimes, rhyme may be used at the start of each line, and although not seen often and frequently missed anyway, this can produce a subtle effect, particularly when paired with end-line rhymes.

Echo Verse

Echo verse is where the final words of each line are shortened, phonetically or literally, and repeated as an "echo" in the line that follows.

For example using shortened words:

> *The dedicated athletes strain*
> *when knowing that they have to train*
> *despite arrival of the rain*

Echo verse reduced phonetically might read:

> *A costly time of Christmas cheer*
> *will come from clearing roads we hear,*
> *with moans that fall upon the ear.*
>
> *Though with the coming of the snow –*
> *there is no way that we can know*
> *how much we later come to owe*

Whilst this is hardly a great poem and is maybe a little contrived, it serves well enough to illustrate the point. It also includes a subtle paired line-start rhyme in the fourth line, but as was previously suggested, you might well be forgiven for not having noticed this.

Clearly, there is more to rhyme than we might at first have thought, and more to be discovered from our own attempts at these various uses. In all cases, however, it will always be the subtlety of rhyme that creates the greatest effect.

GHOSTLY VOWELS

*There is no **A** in a sweet bouquet –*
nor weigh, obey or wild melee.
*There is no **A** found in croquet,*
gourmet, sleigh or chic beret.

*There is no **E** in luxury*
or quay, or even family.
We write with care calligraphy -
*yet cannot find a single **E**.*

*There is, in fact, no **I** in eye...*
nor by, buy, bye or clear blue sky.
*There is no **I** found in deny*
though we might briefly question why?

***O** will be found in words we know*
except a few of foreign source,
like tableau, gateau, faux or beau
or some delightful old chateau.

*There is no **U** in igloo, do or taboo,*
and a rhyming few
like dew and yew, shampoo and who,
which (no doubt) you already knew.

This challenge then, which seems to be
of some elusive subtlety:
how we may hear quite perfectly
these ghostly vowels we fail to see.

Use of Words

Review

We all know what words are and how to use them to express what we want to say, but before moving on to look at the construction of lines and stanzas, this is possibly an opportune moment to pause and consider some of the poetical uses we have already considered.

Our early appreciation of word accent and line stress has shown how words of two or more syllables will have an accentuated part that needs to be maintained when words are used in a line of poetry. We have also seen how the cadence of a line can be modified through the use of various types of meter, and how the meter itself can add emphasis to what is being said. We will later come to see the importance of counting syllables and the effect on metric feet, but for now it is enough to know that words must be seen to fit into the pattern of the meter used.

When considering the sound of words, we have seen how the use, misuse or absence of rhyme can affect the construction of the poem. Words that "chime" have a magic, although there is always a need to ensure that this is a soft and harmonious effect, and not some "sledge-hammer" blow to jar the meaning.

The Sound of Words

The sound of words is always important. It may well be that our awareness of the poetry comes mainly from what we quietly read, and presentation of the poem on the page is frequently a major consideration, but poetry is always meant to be heard.

Indeed, some poems are written specifically as "performance pieces" where a degree of life and energy can be used to enhance and amplify their meaning. We know from our own experience how a poem may sound completely different, depending on who reads it and the manner in which it is read. The use of assonance and alliteration, therefore, can add significantly to the aural appreciation of the poem, in much the same way as the succinct use of rhyme.

Assonance

Assonance is the effect achieved through the deliberate selection and use of similar clear vowel sounds. Such words will not necessarily rhyme, but will define a clear inter-relationship. Take for example an accentuated "e" sound:

> *How easily the evening breeze*
> *will seize the leaves that freely fly.*

An typical example in the use of assonance will be found in later in the poem **"Sonnet of Silver Fire"** *(page 154).*

Alliteration

Alliteration is found in the commencement of words of close proximity, which have the same emphasised consonant sounds. Again, such words may or may not rhyme, but the similarity of sound will be apparent.

Take for example an accentuated "d" sound:

> *Dark the dawn with dismal rain*
> *and dreary daybreak come again.*

The letter "d" is a sharp consonant sound, much like "t" and is clearly noticed. Other softer consonants will tend to be drawn out over a longer length, such as the "s" sound.

> *Soft and slow she sighed and said...*

The combination of assonance and alliteration can be something of a challenge, but will work well if successful. The subtle effect of this can be seen in the poem "**Farmyard Corner**" (page 76)

A deliberate emphasis and slightly archaic result is also shown later in the poem "**Sonnet of Autumn**" (page 83), whilst a more moderate use of alliteration is included in the poem that follows:

THE SILVER SEA

The full moon shone on you last night:
the full moon shone on me.
We softly slept
and sailed across a silent, silver sea.

Yet I awake in that cold light...
in that cold dawning day,
with secrets kept
in dreams, which must as surely fade away.

Sleep on, my love, sleep on this while
upon our silver bed,
and let it be
you softly sail so far away instead.

And let some magic charm beguile
the dreams you journey through
across the sea...
the silver sea,
and take me there with you.

Consonance

Consonance is achieved through the proximity of words that share the same stressed consonant sounds, but where this may occur at any part of the word and where the vowels also differ. For example:

She washes the dishes and splashes her shoes

This may allow a slight play on words, which sound almost the same yet have different meanings. This is shown in the simple poem **"Divided by Time"** (page 77), which illustrates the phonetical similarity of radically different numbers.

FARMYARD CORNER

Beneath the tall and gently swaying nettles,
where terra cotta pots lie lost and broken
and tangled brambles run and root and shoot
and ramble on.
Where musty dampness creeps and slowly settles
on fading sacking, mouldering and soaken –
and left to rot, forgotten...
of some purpose lost and gone.

In hidden mottled shadows slowly drifting
with hazy sunlight filtered soft and mellow,
where caterpillars curl beneath soft leaves
that disappear.
And long, entwining weeds, their thick stems lifting
to flowers, small and bright in shades of yellow –
or thin and jagged petals
turned to puffs of seeded spheres.

A realm of secret, long-abandoned hiding –
a wooden cartwheel blanched by sun and showers
with splintered spokes held fixed
within a rusted iron ring.
And snails in slow procession gently gliding
on gleaming trails of slime,
whilst passing hours
drift undisturbed,
but for a breeze with gentle whispering.

This farmyard corner left for things not needed
and of no value, though they still survive,
and gathered as a history of labour from the past.
A chronicle of yesterdays unheeded,
with worthless relics telling of the lives
of those who come and go...
remembered by such things that last.

DIVIDED BY TIME

You might have been my mistress,
or my lover, or my wife.
I might have been your Romeo...
the true love of your life.

Yet time, it seems, divided all such things
that might have been:
for I, alas, am seventy...
and you are seventeen.

Cliché

If we pause to consider some common adage or saying, we may frequently discover that this has at some time been taken as a short extract from some well-known poem. Such has been the original "impact" of the poem, that a short line or expression has been taken from it, to become absorbed into the English language, along with a unique and implicit meaning. Indeed, the meaning may not, at first glance, be at all obvious, but has come to be "known" initially from the poem, and subsequently accepted through common usage.

Whilst this serves to enrich the English language, its repeated use by us can hardly be regarded as having any originality when writing poetry, and will only undermine our apparent ability to discover something fresh to capture the reader's attention. Consequently, the use of any such cliché or hackneyed phrase, however tempting this might be, is best avoided at all times.

The only possible exception to this general rule may occur when the use of the phrase is deliberate and intended to clearly illustrate the fact that it is well-known. This may express an ironic view of everyday life through the use of a common metaphor, but applied with care, so that we are neither "over the moon" nor "as sick as a parrot" A cliché may be thought of as an example of fossilised poetry, and fossils are for palaeontologists, not poets.

Repetition

The repetition of words in a poem is usually something we try to avoid, particularly when endeavouring to enhance the description of what we want to say. The English language is rich with similar words of a slightly different nuance, and we have only to refer to a modern thesaurus to find them. This may also suggest even more unusual words, which we might not otherwise have thought to use, thereby elevating the poem.

At other times, however, the deliberate repetition of words or even a short phrase can provide emphasis to the poem, and may add a brief pause to help maintain interest and drama. This should not be confused with the use of refrain lines, whose aim is quite different as we will later discover.

LAST OF THE DAYS

*These are the days –
the last of the days.
Days that fade in an autumn haze
and a stroll in the park beneath the trees –
with the leaves: the soft leaves falling.*

*These are the days –
the last of the days,
with silent shadows drifting by.
The pastel greys of a cloudy sky
with the leaves: the soft leaves falling.*

*These are the days –
the last of the days
of solitude and memories.
And a whispering beneath the trees
with the soft leaves –
always the soft leaves gently falling.*

AT THE CLOSE OF DAY

*I will lie with you at the close of day
and smooth our troubled cares away...
at the close of day.*

*I will stay with you in the fading light
and the sudden calm of a peaceful night
at the close of day...at the close of day.*

*I will lie with you. We will mark the rhyme
of our gentle words, at the close of day...
and a gentle time.*

*A time to soothe our cares away
in the peaceful night, and the fading light
of a busy day...such a busy day.*

*I will lie with you, and our thoughts will stray
through the peaceful hours as our cares take flight
and float away...far, far away.*

*And we will share in this calm delight -
for we lose ourselves in the busy day...
lose our way in the busy day
but find ourselves in the night*

Epiphora

Epiphora is the deliberate repetition of words at the start and end of lines, which may occur at regular or irregular intervals. In some more subtle applications, this may include words formed from other partial parts of words which share a phonetic similarity.

For example: hurricanes will often hurry

EPIPHORA

Again...must this be seen again?
Though not too loud should I complain
nor likewise then, try to ignore
foreseen, what I am searching for.
Plain here to see such gain, although
so-written, does it make it so?

Serpentine Verse

Serpentine verse is where a line or stanza of poetry begins and ends with the same word or phrase.

AND SO IT IS

I stay with you
as much from lack of thought as choice –
and of such thoughts we never boldly voice,
I stay with you.

You stay with me
though mainly ignorant or bored
of what, between us, is ignored –
you stay with me.

And so it is
this dull convenience we share –
yet neither notice much nor care:
and so it is.

Archaic Words

It was once thought that poetry had its own form of words and expression: a sort-of blue-print for poetical writing and development. This was possibly derived from an education system, which seemed focused on examples of "classical" poetry, written at a time when everyday language differed significantly from ours.

Considered to be the greatest bard of all time, William Shakespeare (1564 - 1616) is still seen as having achieved the epitome of poetry and use of language. We would be foolish, even today, to question this opinion. His use, therefore, of words such as thee, thou, thine, yore, methinks....and so on, are readily accepted as part of this sincere appreciation and consummate skill of a fine poet. For example, from Sonnet 88 we have the final couplet:

> *"Such is my love, to thee I so belong*
> *That for thy right myself will bear all wrong."*

We must remember, however, that the English language is a living thing... it evolves, adapts and develops with the changing times. Shakespeare wrote in the modern language of his day, and clearly we should do the same.

It is perhaps fortunate that whilst modern education retains a high regard for Shakespeare and his contemporaries, this has broadened to encompass poetry of modern times, of which there are many fine examples. This is poetry with greater relevance to the world of today, and what we write should endeavour to achieve the same.

This is not to say that we might not be tempted, if only for amusement, to try something for ourselves, as the following acrostic sonnet tries to show. This is the element of "poetry for fun" re-asserting itself once more. However, when we do so, let's at least make it obvious that we know what we are doing!

VALENTINE RHYME

Vowed e'er to be of constant charm and grace,
As strove they thus who wouldst of favour be -
Likewise whereof I liefer then doth place
Enchantment goodly writ in poetry.
Not that I hath erstwhile a grimly task,
That might in dolour of mine time be wroth.
It be that I, unbade, doth wherefore ask
Nought else but that I bare to thee my troth.
E'er were I ware of thy true love, long since,
Rose hath no beauty fairer then than thee -
Hereafter thus behove I be thy prince,
Yet wouldst as servant serve unto thy plea.
My life be thus foresworn and gainsay be
E'er to thy bidding; as be thine of me.

By way of translation into "modern" English the previous poem reads as follows:

Promising to be true as others
who wish to win your approval,
I prefer to write you an enchanting poem.
Not that this is a grim task, which I might regret,
since I would hope to show my love for you.
From the time I first met you,
I have admired your beauty
and wished to become your prince,
yet would be happy to do whatever you might ask.
This is my declared aim:
to live for you and have you live for me.

I think, somehow, that it sounds better in early Elizabethan English!

The use of assonance and alliteration, whilst adding a charming quality to the poem, can sometimes appear slightly archaic if applied in an excessive way, as the following sonnet shows:

SONNET OF AUTUMN

When autumn's awesome cloak of beauty bold
returns like burnished copper to the trees;
unfolds in golden splendour uncontrolled
the endless charm of blending harmonies.
When peaceful calm and haunting melodies,
drift in a mystic haze of rustic praise,
from whispers in the gentle evening breeze
and dormant grace, embraced in warm displays.
When autumn fills the still and lazy days
with skill that will defy the artist's eye,
and paints the changing season this portrays
in timeless beauty, rhyme cannot deny.
So too when growing old, to then behold
the spread of autumn years with threads of gold

Allusion

Allusion is when a poem alludes to another, but in an obvious manner. This acknowledgement pays respect to the former author by not seeking to take-on any reflected glory or suggestion of plagiarism. To achieve this will require that the poem echoes in some way an aspect of the former poem, but that it should also add some new perspective; some new thought or direction.

Poetry is the voice of the poet with something to say. The thought or idea that inspires the poem may not be original in itself, but in terms of expressing this the poet must also find words to show something personal felt inside... and that will always be unique.

The example poem that follows includes a deliberate allusion made from partial reference to possibly the best-remembered poems by three famous poets:

"Adlestrop" by Edward Thomas (1878 - 1917),
"The Road Not Taken" by Robert Frost (1874 - 1963),
"The Listeners" by Walter de la Mere (1873 - 1956).

Clearly the reader might need to have had some prior knowledge of these three poems, although this is not an essential part of the new poem created from these references, where the final stanza provides its own final conclusion.

ADLESTROP DENIED

This will not be my Adlestrop,
for I have not come here to pause
and view success. I cannot stop
when governed by more subtle laws
than mere ambition as the cause.

This is not where two paths diverge
that I may choose the lesser one.
The promises I keep must urge,
my journey on: the prize not won
that sees some special poem done.

I am the stranger seeking here
to hammer on the moonlit door
and know of ghosts that linger near -
for I have come this way before
in search of truth and wanting more.

Yet shall I ever know the deed?
It matters not should I not see
one poem... just the one, perceived
the best of many prized by me.
Held by such value, let it be
that others may some pleasure find
from words that I will leave behind.

Another form of allusion might be to "adopt" the specific theme of a poem and consider this under alternative circumstances. For example, in the poem "Adlestrop" by Edward Thomas (1878 - 1917) he speaks of a train making an unscheduled stop during a typical summer's day.

Let us then suppose that the traveller returns once more to Addlestrop but in winter time. How might this change in circumstances influence the experience of the journey?

ADLESTROP IN WINTER

If I had not been here before,
then might I have remained unsure
of having come to where I wished to be.

Reluctant now to leave the train,
where I might otherwise remain
cocooned in warmth and friendly company.

Yet here I was, and here once more
I opened wide the carriage door,
and stepping out into the cold night air.

A gust of wind tugged at my coat:
a swirl of leaves, that seemed to float
along the empty platform, cold and bare.

And here again, to this bleak place
chilled with the grey of winter's grace
of distant solitude and gathering gloom.

Dull clouds bruised with a promised rain:
the sound of the departing train
and faint-lit comfort from the waiting room.

How is it then that thoughts betray
such times that dwell, though far away,
when first I came by train to visit here.

The days long-past remembered then
in Adlestrop one summer, when
the birds sang and the sky shone blue and clear.

Whilst most allusion poems tend to adopt an idea or perhaps a brief phrase, some may be taken a step further, with complete lines or phrases taken from one or more poems by a famous poet. Again, the source of such lines should be made obvious to avoid any hint of plagiarism, either within the context of the new poem or in subsequent notes.

The poem that follows was written following a visit to Woburn Walk, a small cobbled walkway in London, where the poet William Butler Yates (1865 - 1939) lived from 1895 to 1919.

References to poems by Wiliam Butler Yates (1865 - 1939) are as follows:

1. **The Lake Isle of Innisfree**
   "... nine bean rows will I have there,
   a hive for the honey bee
   and live in the bee-loud glade"
2. "... while I stand on the roadway,
   or on pavements grey
3. I hear it in the deep heart's core"
4. **He Wishes For The Cloths Of Heaven**
   "Tread softly because you tread on my dreams"
5. **The Song Of The Wandering Aengus**
6. "The silver apples of the moon,
   the golden apples of the sun."
7. **When You Are Old**
   "When you are old and grey and full of sleep"

It is not always necessary to know or even provide sources of lines in an allusion poem, although clearly this may be of added interest to the reader when possible, perhaps in the form of notes as shown above.

The importance, of course, is not to attempt to pass off the words of some great poet as one's own.

WOBURN WALK

His window overlooked the cobbled walk
where cherry blossom, touched by morning light,
floated like tissue in the city breeze.
From cafe tables shaded by the trees,
in pools of dappled sunshine, came the bright
soft murmur of old friends and idle talk.

Perhaps at times he too was tempted down
to join with them and while away an hour
in friendly conversation – then retire
back to his room with words that would inspire
thoughts of some bee-loud glade
where bean rows flower [1]
far from the pavements grey of London town . [2]

And through the late and drowsy afternoon
his gentle soft rhyme patterns given birth
to softly tread through dreams and slip away [4]
with golden apples of the fading day. [6]
A melody of words whose measured worth
remained like silver apples of the moon. [5]

The years have drifted by, though Woburn Walk
remains unchanged, as does his window view.
No longer old and grey and full of sleep [7]
it seems his ghost remains, as if to keep
the memory of all that he once knew:
bright laughter and the murmur of soft talk

and lingering to touch the days once more
and hear it in the deep heart's core. [3]

Cento

The cento (from the Latin "patchwork") is also a form of allusion poetry, but is made up entirely from lines and phrases taken from other famous poems, written by any number of poets. Often this is presented in the form of free verse, since the matching of rhyme and meter from so many sources becomes an increasingly difficult challenge.

Aside from the need to link this assortment of lines, the general aim is also to provide such known lines or phrases with a twist, so that they may assume some new meaning. A simple "cobbling-together" of lines will hardly warrant any literary merit unless there is some new interest in them. In recent times, the lines taken from well-known songs may also be considered as an alternative to those taken from poems, possibly with a more immediate sense of recognition.

Parody

The parody is an imitative work intended to satirize or trivialise an original poem. It may often be quite sarcastic in its approach, and will seek to focus on a particular aspect of the poem - perhaps the style or subject. On a more personal level (as is often the case) it may target the poet. If done in a light-hearted or jocular fashion this may be termed a spoof, although often the intention is to lampoon the person in some way.

Pastiche

The pastiche is a specific type of literary allusion, which may not necessary accept any of the thoughts or emotions of the original, but seeks instead to extract a specific quality and emulate this in an amusing manner.

This may, for example, take the form of bringing a classic poem sharply into the 21st century, with all of the anomalies that this might create. Alternatively, the pastiche may simply transpose a particular and distinctive element of a famous poem into a new situation.

Take, for example, "The Song of Hiawatha" written by Henry Wadsworth Longfellow (1807 - 1882) in a very distinctive trochaic meter, and applied a more modern experience:

BRIGHTON DAYS (OF SUN AND SUNSHINE)

By the shores of Hove and Brighton,
by the bright and shining shingle -
there beside the deep sea water
where the old pier once went right on
out to sea, when I was single.
By the salty, seaside shoreline
when the days were warm and made fine
in the summer sunshine passing -
memories I would not alter
long ago... and young and golden.

How it was, in days now olden
from the yesterdays long faded
of the summer sunshine passing -
faded and forgotten mostly,
or like ancient photo's ghostly.
Distant images and jaded,
though I would remember gladly
times of youth and bold invention -
things of love that I might mention,
though I do recall them badly.

By the shores of Hove and Brighton,
and a time of friends and laughter -
how it was with a delight on
sunny days, and bright sea water.
Greetings then, with "Hiya Walter!"
"Let's go swimming, and then after
at the discotheque go dancing."
Sunny weather, filled with sunlight
and such happy times enhancing,
and romancing in the moonlight.

Ever young and ever youthful,
though it was (if I am truthful)
that I longed then to be older -
see the world and likewise shoulder
my awareness, never knowing
all too soon I would be growing
with a longed-for wish once more mine
of a distant time beholden,
just to walk along the shoreline
when my days were young and golden.

A Final Word on Words

English, as a language, is a living thing and as such it is continuously evolving and changing. In many instances this may reflect changes in society, where new words become necessary to express a unique situation. An example might be the word "dinky" used to describe a young couple... "dual income, no kids yet".

The word "partners" is another example, which has become universally accepted as a means of describing two people who live together, whilst have decided not to get married. At one time, of course, such behaviour would have seemed morally reprehensible, but changes in society and accepted behaviour requires a similar change in language to describe this. We might possible apply this same view to the present modern use of the word "gay", which has all but lost its original meaning of bright and colourful.

Language has always been used by factions of society keen to establish their own identity, and may apply some completely new meaning to existing words. Such things tend to come and go quite quickly, like small bubbles floating briefly in time, although other words may gain widespread appeal throughout a larger spectrum.

There is clearly a temptation, possibly a need, to include this use of language in poetry, especially if we wish to place the poem into a particular modern social environment.

The only cautionary note to this is that, much like the changing use of words, the poem will become locked into this time-frame. What was at one time "with it" in terms of meaning and understanding is, with the passage of time, sadly without it once more. The use of more conventional words, whilst lacking a particular sparkle, will never-the-less acquire a more ageless quality.

One other aspect of writing is a temptation to invent words... it's all part of the fun. Some new word may suggest itself, and provided that it can be used in context, thereby giving a clue to its meaning, then why not?

The poem **"Farmyard Corner"** (page 76) included the following line:

"on fading sacking, mouldering and soaken –"

I will readily confess that this provided a convenient rhyme to "broken" but taken in context it also added to the description of the saturated sacking in a way that was clearly understood. The poet seeks to find his or her own voice, and the discovery of new words is surely an integral part of this.

A Living Language

Finally, there is always good cause to consider the origin of modern English, which has evolved on a small island, frequently conquered by various invaders such as the Vikings, Celtic tribes, Romans, Saxons and the Normans... to name but a few. On each occasion these "foreigners" have brought with them a wealth of new words and use of language, readily absorbed into everyday conversation.

No other language in the world reflects this more than English, with its duality of expression, its idiosyncratic spelling and its often obscure derivation of words, which makes it one of the most difficult languages to learn. Greek and Latin influences are many, and manifest themselves through a classical foundation from which our English has evolved. These are seen in examples of the far-from-obvious spelling challenges that beset any scholar when learning English, as well as a confusion with some plurals of words.

A former expansion of the British Empire has resulted in the spread of English throughout the world, where (through the partial isolation of other countries) it has continued to evolve and diverge. We have only to compare differences between America and England to be reminded how quickly such changes can occur.

By way of an amusing example, the following poems explore one aspect of the classical origin of words through the uncertainty of a correct plural:

OCTOPUS PUZZLE

The octopus poses a problem
apart from its size and its shape.
It's the name then, you see,
and will no doubt agree,
which offers us little escape.

It began with the Greeks (as so many things do)
and the "oktopous" that they once knew –
from which we expect
octopodes is correct,
should we be referring to two.

Octopodes is archaic, said scholars –
octopus is from Latin derived,
and though we might try
to apply octopi,
this is wrong...though has strangely survived.

So if, in the course of discussion,
we might feature a creature or two,
in etymological fashion
octopuses correctly will do...

while rhinoceros and hippopotamus
are, perhaps, better left in the zoo.

DOUBLE TROUBLE

The Romans and the Greeks, it seems,
caused language problems in extremes -
with plurals never quite what we
might otherwise expect to see.

There's foot and feet... a man and men:
ox and oxen... mouse and mice.
There's tooth and teeth, a goose and geese.
Such rules, indeed, need some advice.

This and that are these and those.
More than a penny then is pence.
One half.... two halves: one loaf...two loaves,
though none of this makes any sense.

Addendum and addenda match
with datum...data, such is so.
Person and people, wife and wives -
such are the plurals we should know.

Some items have no single form
of which we may be well aware:
pants and trousers, scissors, glasses -
always spoken as a pair.

How pleasant also are the words
where just an "s" will then suffice
to make from one the many more,
with not a hint of die and dice.

Or better yet, the chosen few
of rare examples, which then keep
a constant word... such praise indeed
for species, aircraft, fish and sheep.

The play on words can result in great amusement, particularly when focussed on the anomalies that exist. The normal ability to form a plural by adding an "s" clearly does not apply in a great many exceptions, which must be learnt for what they are, as the previous poem illustrates:

Some poets, such as Roger McGough (1937 -), are also noted for the way that they are able to run words together to create clever puns which, though subtle, are quite clearly understood. It is interesting to try something similar in this example:

OURTIME

It is ourtime now:
ourtime of rest and retaxation
with justapension to see us through.

Our freefrom harmhouse in the sun –
growing tomatoes and daydreams
through the fundays and satalldays
long awaited.

Taking each day at a rhyme
and reason enough for a restawhile
in the passing of ourtime
and happy ever laughter.

Use of English Language

There are many aspects of the English language that are learnt, not from books, but through common usage. We hear and quickly adopt certain subtleties of language into our speech, with scarcely a thought as to the way in which this happens. Language is a living thing, and will change in many ways, either through the introduction of new words or, indeed, a changed meaning and usage of existing words.

As previously mentioned, words such as "cool" (meaning laid-back) or "wicked" (meaning good or excellent) are readily used in modern conversation, yet may as quickly fade once more as time and trends move on.

This may occur without any great conscious effort, whereby we will likewise adapt and find new meaning in words and phrases, in much the same way as clichés (which may often have no clear literal meaning) are readily understood and accepted.

It is as well, however, to understand what it is we are doing. Here are a few of the more common uses of language:

Personification

This is when an inanimate object is attributed with human characteristics, and may help to embellish or attribute the said object with some added charm. For example:

"The flower smiled at the sun".

Metonymy

Often used in poetry, this is when an object is substituted by a word that alludes to some general attribute or concept. For example:

"The castle belonged to the crown"

Synecdoche

Limiting the description of something by describing just some particular aspect. For example:

"Her golden hair and lilting laugh won all men's hearts"

Litotes

The use of an understatement or negative to give added emphasis. For example:

"He wasn't half-bad at playing football"

Hyperbole

The use of exaggeration for added effect. For example:

"She was a divine angel"

Onomatopoeia

The formation of words or a brief phrase which phonetically imitates or is immediately associated with the object being described. For example:

"The tiger growled and the cat meowed...each understood the other.

The proper use of English grammar may sometimes criticise this common use of language as little better than slang. However, when writing poetry it is as well to remember that the use of modern language can help to place the poem within a current context. The only note of caution, perhaps, is that the use of some expressions may come and go quite quickly, in which case the poem will then appear dated.

The Length of Lines

Review

Words are made up from one or more syllables, which can be regarded as units of pronunciation forming the complete word. Each such unit will usually include a vowel sound, with consonants that proceed or follow the vowel. In some ways, a syllable can be seen as the smallest part of speech, and it is hardly surprising to discover that a vast number of the words we use have just one syllable.

Words of two or more syllables will be seen to have an accent: an emphasis on part of the word at some natural position, in keeping with normal conversation. We have already looked at this accent and the way in which it needs to be considered carefully when writing a line of poetry, which will itself have stresses at regular intervals, according to the form of meter being used.

From a previous example of two-syllable words, "shining" and "brightly" are spoken as "**shi**-ning" and "**bright**-ly" with the emphasis (accent) on the start of the words. Quite often, words of two or more syllables may lose their normal accent in favour of the line stress, but may never be in conflict with it.

Clearly, the longer the word, the greater number of syllables we may expect it to have. For example "denominational" and "egocentricity" have six syllables and other words like "autobiographical" have seven. It is probably true to say that the longer the words we use, the greater becomes the challenge to fit them into a metrical line of poetry.

For example, we might fit "autobiographical" into a *trochaic* meter, although it would sound stilted.

"**aut**-o-**bi**-o-**graph**-i-**cal** im-**press**-ions"
***TUM**-ti **TUM**-ti **TUM**-ti **TUM**-ti **TUM**-ti*

Normal speech would tend to move quicker than this and when written would probably be achieved with combined *paeon, dactylic and amphibrachic* meters:

"**Aut**obio- **graph**ical im-**press**ions"
***TUM**-ti-ti-ty **TUM**-ti-ty ti-**TUM** -ty*

Whether by accident or intention, some lesser-known Greek meters may also be used in lines of mixed meter (see page 265)

If this is starting to sound complicated, simply forget the names but observe how the stresses occur along the line. In the trochaic meter we had five stresses along the line, whereas in the mixed meter example above we now have only three feet. The poem now moves quicker and in a more natural way as a result

Measuring The Line

Some poetry is written with a strict regard to the number of syllables in each line...and why not? It is as good a way as any to apply such a simple rule, and the results can be rewarding.

The ancient art of haiku - a form of Japanese poetry, relies purely on the counting of syllables with just three lines of 5, 7 and 5 syllables. Having no requirement of rhyme or meter, this may sound remarkably easy, yet it is far from being so as we will later discover.

For the moment, however, let us consider a more typical line of poetry, which is written with a regular meter. Such a line will be divided into feet, which take account of the number of stresses along its length.

For example:

"The garden is lovely this bright summer's day"
"The **gar**den is **love**ly this **bright** sum mer's **day**"
*(ti-**TUM**-ty, ti-**TUM**-ty, ti-**TUM**-ty, ti-**TUM**)*

There are four stresses along the line, which is consequently divided into four feet. This is said to be a tetrameter line of poetry (in mixed amphibrachic and iambic meter). A line of poetry may be as short or as long as we wish it to be, although we will frequently find that writing in a natural way tends to result in lines of four or five feet.

For example:

> *"We know a sonnet must have fourteen lines"*
> "We **know** a **sonn**et **must** have **four**teen **lines**"
> *(ti-**TUM**, ti-**TUM**, ti-**TUM**, ti-**TUM**, ti-**TUM**)*

We also know that a sonnet should be written in iambic pentameter, which is what the above example shows.

Finding the Length

The use of short lines can often provide a sharp, almost precise effect to the poem, giving the impression of a brief outline and allowing the reader to colour-in the spaces. Short lines, particularly when interspersed between longer lines, can also create a dramatic effect.

Any attempt at writing longer lines of poetry (usually when exceeding six feet) is often fraught with difficulty, since the natural tendency will be for these lines to disintegrate into shorter lengths. It can be done, but will normally require a fast pace which prevents any pause along the middle of such a line.

Naming the Lines

It is as well to know the names, as follows:

monometer	**1** foot	*sometimes used for dramatic effect*
dimeter	**2** feet	*seen between longer lines*
trimeter	**3** feet	*sharp and succinct use*
tetrameter	**4** feet	*frequent use*
pentameter	**5** feet	*frequent use*

OLD AGE AND NEW DAYS

I find the days have not been too unkind,
although they do exact a measured price
from memories of time too quickly gone.
Reminded of the dreams I leave behind –
though dawns a bright tomorrow to entice
renewed desire... a sense of moving on.

The nimbleness of thought that never dims,
though limbs grow weary sometimes, needing rest.
The pace now slower than it was before –
yet able to achieve from passing whims
what can be done, and so to make the best
of all that waits ahead left to explore.

And of old age, no change brought into view
that sees the minted day dawn bright and new.

The ubiquitous iambic pentameter is known as a heroic line, so that two such lines become a heroic couplet and four such lines stanza gives us the heroic stanza.

The iambic pentameter has always been a popular choice, since it closely follows normal speech. Certain classical forms of poetry, such as the sonnet, have always traditionally used this format, although some modern variations are possible, as we will later see.

Continuing on, we begin to discover quite lengthy lines and an increasing inflexibility

hexameter   **6** feet   *occasional considered use*

The Alexandrine is a line of iambic hexameter, and if tried will begin to demonstrate the increasing temptation to divide such lines into smaller lengths. For example:

> *The **length** of **lines** should **not** exceed what **comes** to **be**
> as **much** as **any** writer then would **like** to see.*

heptameter   **7** feet   *rarely used and with difficultly*

To achieve 7 feet in a single line might be possible for an iambic heptameter, although this would tend to "gallop" along. If, however, a poem was written in anapaestic meter, the sheer volume of words jammed into each line might become difficult, if not impossible. Imagine also the problem in trying to recite such a line with the need for a pause somewhere along the way:

> *From the **inco**nse**quen**tial di**vi**sion of **lines** into **feet**
> we can **clear**ly ex**plain**,
> how the ex**ten**ded **lines** have be**come** broken **down**
> into **eas**ier **short** lengths a**gain**.*

Any attempt to write using iambic heptameter would still show a tendency to divide the lines, if only to improve the meaning.

An example follows showing how some of the longer lines can remain as such, whilst others are better divided, partly through the occurrence of natural pauses and use of punctuation, and also through a need to add clarity.

STRANGERS

> *She cannot quite recall now
> how she came to this new place –
> the memory of yesterday has faded without trace.
> She wonders who these strangers are
> that visit her each day?
> They smile and say a few kind words
> and then they go away,
> though they bring her cards and flowers,
> and they seem to know her name.
> They come and stay a while,
> although she wonders why they came,
> or why it is they seem so sad
> and why they sometimes cry –
> hesitating by the door, before they say goodbye.*

It is difficult to perceive what advantage might be gained from using lines that exceed the heptameter in length

octometer   **8** feet   *Used with great difficulty and with lines often divided*

                     BIEN DANS SA PEAU
                     (Comfortable in your skin)

                     It is enough...
                     this measure shared of dreams become reality;
                     of having wished for change and dared
                     to trust in such ability.

                     It is enough...
                     though it may grow a greater truth we see fulfilled;
                     some greater aim we come to know
                     of new achievements that we build.

                     It is enough... these days that bring
                     both work and ease in measures found,
                     and of such love as poet's sing
                     our days with harmony now crowned.

                     It is enough...
                     bien dans sa peau, that finds us of a simple aim
                     whatever words be used,
                     to know such thoughts translated are the same.

A poem that combines words or phrases in different languages is known as Macaronic verse. We will consider this in more detail later (see page 206).

The octometer is generally regarded as the longest line possible in the formal classification of lines, although (theoretically) longer line lengths are possible.

In most cases, when read aloud it will be found that normal speech requires a few pauses at mid-positions along the way, usually where necessary punctuation also indicates a need to pause.

As these increasingly stretched lines start to show, we are beginning to reach a limit with regards to our ability to write or read these longer lines in a normal manner.

| nonometer | **9** feet | *a highly improbable use* |
| decameter | **10** feet | *ambitious and probably impossible* |

Keeping a check

Writing is generally a spontaneous and creative activity. The initial aim is usually focussed on getting a sudden idea down on paper in some personal and original manner that makes sense.

Any form of art, whether it be painting, writing, composing music, dancing... whatever medium is used, any form of art is concerned primarily with communication. Initially, therefore, what is required is the inspiration necessary for a new way of communicating or expressing this.

The old maxim of 10% inspiration and 90% perspiration may not always be quite accurate, but is certainly of an approximately correct ratio. The hardest part, however, is often found in seeking out that all-important initial spark, from which the process of creating a poem can begin. This may often arrive quite unexpectedly and with little warning, so always having pen and paper nearby is clearly a good idea.

It is only later, with the early draft of a poem in hand, that we may start to consider the technical merit of what we have written. Does it scan? Do the words flow? Does it have a good use of meter, and is there some sense of order to the length of lines? At this point we may even start to count feet!

It might well be that the lines differ significantly, and when writing in free verse this is probably what is intended. Line breaks will occur at natural pauses, perhaps, or at moments when the poet wishes to emphasise a particular thought before moving on.

However, if we are intent on using some traditional form of poetry, then it is as well that we begin to keep a check on where we are heading.

The poet who intends to write a sonnet or villanelle does not come across these forms by accident. There is no serendipity which allows some inspired thought to manifest itself in a particular stanza or controlled arrangement other than, perhaps, simple couplets or four-line stanzas, usually in an iambic meter and with a simple rhyme scheme.

At an early stage, therefore, a critical assessment of the technical qualities of the poem needs to be made. This has very little to do with artistic merit, which we may come to view at a later time. Indeed, the desired aesthetic nature of the poem may well mean that we sacrifice something of the technical merit: an imperfect rhyme, perhaps, or a slightly irregular meter. Better a rough diamond than polished glass!

At the start, however, we should endeavour to pay some attention to the type of poem we hope to write, using what we have learnt so far with regard to stress and accent, as well as the use of meter and an awareness of syllables and the lengths of lines.

Knowing this will not, necessarily, help us write excellent poetry, which must always come from any inherent talent we have spoken of before in the introduction to this book. However, knowing how to handle words and lines of poetry will help to improve what is written and give rise to something of harmony and movement.

It will also develop an appreciation of the talent shown by many of the famous and contemporary poets we read from time to time. We can learn a great deal from such enjoyment and observation.

Stanza Forms

Introduction

From our introduction to stanzas, it is apparent that we may expect a strict requirement for the arrangement of lines in traditional forms of poetry. For some writers, the completion of a poem to such a set of requirements will add a sense of added achievement, whilst others will see this as too restrictive.

Quite often it may be found that the first stanza (of however many lines) will arrive in a particular rhyme pattern. The challenge then will be to repeat this pattern in the number of stanzas that follow, so that the complete poem shows a structure with a very clear identity.

In any attempt to write poetry, it is essential that the writer must also find what best suits the way a particular poem is to be expressed. For many poets, writing is a spontaneous activity, and the thought of any prior planning with regards to stanza patterns and use of stanzas will not be a viable proposition. For others, the start of a poem may well suggest the framework of a traditional poem, and this will then serve to plan and assist in what is to be expressed.

Stanza Considerations

For traditional forms of poetry, the construction of stanzas will be dictated by four main considerations:

    1 The number of lines per stanza , which is usually fixed.
    2 The type of meter, which may sometimes vary.
    3 The number of feet per line, which may also vary.
    4 The rhyme pattern for the lines, which may or may not be dictated by the type of traditional poem chosen, and may even include the use of refrain lines.

Refrain Lines

It may seem odd to begin our study of stanza forms by looking at a single line, but the single refrain line has a habit of appearing in the most unexpected places, so it is as well at the start to prepare ourselves for this! The refrain line in a poem is usually a complete line, which is repeated to provide added emphasis.

Certain forms of traditional verse will use refrain lines as a chorus, reminding us of a time when ballads were sung, rather than recited as poems. Sometimes it may be just a phrase from the line that is repeated.

The modern use of refrain lines also allows some slight variations to the line or phrase, which may be done to good effect. Whether a true refrain or one where minor changes are made, the effect will always be noticeable.

IN THE PASSING OF THE DAYS

In the passing of the days:
the rising and the setting sun –
we come to know, in many ways
the loving moments we have won
in the passing of the days.

In the passing of the nights:
the warmth when you lie close to me,
and all of constant love's delights
we share in gentle harmony
in the passing of the nights.

In the passing of the years:
the days and nights remembered well.
The love we share, that life appears
enchanted with a magic spell
in the passing of the years.

In the previous example, a refrain line has been used at the start and finish of each stanza, and has then been modified slightly from one stanza to the next, which tends to unify the complete poem. Refrain lines may be used as complete stanzas, particularly at the start and finish of a poem, where perhaps some slight change can add a whole new meaning, as shown in the following example:

OVER OCEAN DEPTHS

*My love has travelled a thousand miles –
a thousand miles and more,
and far away where now she smiles
beside a distant shore.*

*The sun that shines on my love today
will likewise shine on me,
though thoughts can never sail away
that linger constantly.*

*As here I watch for the turning tide
and waves that kiss the shore –
this longing that I cannot hide,
she might return once more.*

*The ocean depths swirl dark and green
that I may never cross –
the cold and wind-chilled waves between
that measure now my loss.*

*My love has travelled a thousand miles –
a thousand miles of sea,
and far away where now she smiles
but does not think of me.*

Another use the refrain line is to transpose it slightly. In the example that follows a simple rhyme scheme: **abab bcbc**
has had the first line changed to give a modified
refrain in the form of a final couplet: **abab bcbcc**

The rhyme scheme: **abab bcbcc**   is known as a Spenserian stanza (see page 140)

FRUSTRATION

*The ink is too black and the page is too white
and my thoughts, seeking words,
                    are uncertain and grey,
with little of clarity that I might write –
like a mistiness shrouding the dawning of day.
Such thoughts that grow vague
                    and found drifting away
from all bright inspiration, which I seem to lack.
These words...these few words,
                    which yet fail to convey
the frustration of wandering lost on a track
where the page is too white,
                    and the ink is too black.*

The Random Refrain

There is no reason to suppose that refrain lines will occur only at the end of stanzas or that they may not be modified slightly.

The poem that follows has been written in the form of a terza rima. We will come to look at this stanza form later (see page 124), but for now we need only focus on the positioning of the refrain lines. These have been placed in such a way that the 2nd line of one stanza is repeated in the 3rd line of the stanza that follows. The poem also "completes a loop" so that following this convention the final stanza becomes a repeat of the first stanza.

Expressed using our convention of letters to represent rhymes and upper case to show refrain lines we have...

A^1BA bCB cDC dED eFE fGF gAG A^1BA

DAWN RISING

She rises as the night stars fade
and dresses for the coming day –
her mood by colours then displayed.

At times she wears a misty grey
or primrose shades of palest hue,
when dressing for the coming day.

At other times, a cloudy blue,
which hints at hazy fields and trees –
their distant shades of palest hue.

Yet sometimes bolder by degrees –
like ocean currents, deep and green,
seen in the summer fields and trees.

And sometimes in grim colours seen –
grey as a storm and darker still
than ocean chasms, deep and green.

Though she may also dress to thrill
in fiery reds that brightly glow
after a storm, when all is still.

But often, as her mood may show,
in pastel colours then displayed
with warming reds that gently glow.

She rises as the night stars fade
and dresses for the coming day –
her mood by colours then displayed.

It should be noted in the above poem that this slightly complicated construction is quite unique. A terza rima poem in itself would be seen as a recognisable construction, without the additional positioning "non-conventional" modified refrain lines.

The mixing of different elements of a poem may, in fact, often go unnoticed, and in any event should not be made too or obvious or allow to interfere with the desired flow of words.

Couplets

Couplets are the easiest form of rhyme to achieve and can be readily modified as the poem progresses.

BLUE TIT GREETING

An autumn dawn and with it, without warning,
comes sudden noise to stir this fair, good morning.
I rise to see the cedar tree, from where
a boisterous sound of birdsong fills the air.

The sun, though barely risen through the chill
of morning mist, and moon that lingers still,
sheds pearly light across a cloudless sky,
where now a flock of blue tits brightly fly.

Yet as to how or why – then who may know
what causes them, this day, to gather so?
A dozen and a dozen...maybe more
that chirp and chatter, flutter...scatter...soar.

The farmer, busy through the recent days
has gathered-in his harvest now of maize,
and well it may be blue tits come to find
some bounty left of seeds he leaves behind.

Though at the start, it seems that this must be
a time to gather in the cedar tree.
This cheerful throng that comes to sing and play
with their bright greeting, this September day.

If we consider the epic work of Geoffrey Chaucer (1343–1400) we find that the Canterbury Tales were written entirely in couplets, to allow the stories to flow and develop.

Shakespeare's plays also include couplets for a similar reason, as well as aiding actors when it comes to remembering their lines! Clearly they will work as well for us.

Couplets combined with a strong paeon meter (ti-ti-**TUM**-ty), can create quite a forceful tone, which drives the poem along in a somewhat strident manner.

The performance poem that follows is intended to be read with a slightly commanding accent, reminiscent perhaps a former army colonel. It is not intended as a stereotype of any such military men, but works to suggest a slightly intolerant attitude in what is intended to be an amusing way.

AT THE START

At the start I wasn't bothered – couldn't really give a damn
if I did or if I didn't... that's the sort of chap I am.

For a while I thought about it, not quite sure what I should do –
then decided, what the hell, perhaps I might just see it through.

Not convinced it was essential: not a case of "do or die".
More a view of "here we go". A chance, maybe, to have a try.

But it seemed procrastination had resulted in a change:
and the offer now withdrawn
although I found the reason strange.

Now things denied become attractive – this, I find, is often so.
Things illicit...pagan...tempting soon take on a rosy glow.

So it came as no surprise that I should then be soon aware
how this former mild ambition had a charged, determined air.

I wanted it...I needed it: desire and lust had come alive.
Certain as I was, without it doubting that I could survive.

Too late...too late!
The chance had gone held forfeit to my brief delay.
Oh woe...cried I (or something stronger)
in my sudden stark dismay.

Black the clouds with promised thunder –
dark the depths of my despair.
Had I ever known such sorrow?
Had I ever known such care?

It passed, of course...it drifted by,
was soon forgotten where it lay.
I rose to face a bright new future and an even brighter day.

And just by chance there came an offer –
something different and quite new.
Though at first I wasn't bothered...
thought I'd wait a day or two.

The Ballad Stanza

The ballad stanza has four lines with a rhyme scheme: **abab**.
It is what most people think of as a typical stanza. Sometimes it may be that only lines 2 and 4 are seen to rhyme, which is even easier! Strictly speaking the 1st and 3rd lines are written in iambic tetrameter (4 feet) whilst the 2nd and 4th lines are in iambic trimeter (3 feet).

WHERE SINGS THE WREN

*Beneath a bush beside the hedge
that runs along the lane –
where sings the wren but briefly and
then disappears again.*

*Where late the wild rose flowers with
a pale and ghostly hue,
and on and on across the fields
a distant misty view.*

*Above the blackened branches of
the ancient apple tree,
the sombre clouds of dull November
passing casually -*

*and fallen fruit of russet orbs
decaying in the grass,
where cattle come to graze and stare
and hours slowly pass.*

*Beyond the lane that wanders where
the stone-built farmhouse stands,
and all of long-forgotten time
that seeps into these lands.*

*In quiet contemplation come
where we will now remain,
and listen as the wren returns
to sing to us again.*

The ballad as a poem may include any number of stanzas. In the medieval days of wandering minstrels these would serve as a source of news and events up and down the country, growing in length as more information was added. The ballad became a "living thing" and was readily adapted with older news slowly replaced by modern events.

Modern poetry will allow all manner of variations in meter when using the accepted ballad stanza: **abab**

The following poem has an added couplet: **ab**
to give a sonnet of fourteen lines.

KNOWN BY CATS

The cats know we are leaving -
how this is so I cannot say,
though pointless in deceiving
we will soon be on our way.

They show no signs of grieving -
that we will go and they must stay.
Content enough believing
we will return another day.

Yet still they watch, achieving
a sense of guilt, which they convey.
How we might go, perceiving
a trust, which somehow we betray.

With mixed emotions weaving:
it's just a holiday we say,
in hope to be achieving
their understanding, if we may.

The cats know we are leaving –
how this is so I cannot say.

Rubai (plural Rubaiyat)

The rubai is another four-line stanza with a rhyme pattern: **aa-a**. This gives three rhyming lines and a non-rhyming third line.

Rubaiyat may be written using any meter, although it is not surprising to see the frequent use of an iambic meter once more. The length of lines and number of feet may also vary, and the poem may also have any number of stanzas.

The best known example is probably the Rubaiyat of Omar Khayyam (1048 - 1131), as translated by Edward FitzGerald (1809 - 1883). The rubaiyat is less popular than might be supposed, although some modern poems can be found. Since the stanza form has a relative simplicity, it is possible (although not necessary) to interlink stanzas in various ways.

This is seen in the poem "Stopping by Woods on a Snowy Evening" by Robert Frost (1874 - 1963), and the rhyme scheme used:

aaba, bbcb, ccdc, ddDD

Note: Using our convention to indicate rhyme endings with letters, refrain lines are shown in upper case, but rhyme with other lines in lower case of the same letter.

It is known that Robert Frost had originally intended the final stanza to be **dded** (as expected), but this left him with more to add beyond the third line, which was where he felt the poem should stop. His decision, therefore, was to simply repeat this line, which was to give the poem a lasting impact from the unexpected refrain. What he had done, in effect, was to bend the rules to suit the poem, rather than the other way around.

The woods are lovely, dark and deep,
but I have promises to keep
and miles to go before I sleep
and miles to go before I sleep"

Rubaiyat are sometimes written to "close the loop" often by having the penultimate line "echo" the first line, thus:

Aaba, bbcb, ccdc, ddAd

Another alternative sometimes favoured in the rubaiyat is to have the normally non-rhyming third line of each stanza linked by a common rhyme thus:
aaxa, bbxb, ccxc, and so on.

Clearly there are many such options by which a simple stanza form can be linked with others into the final poem.

SEA VIEW RUBAIYAT

I am drawn to the sea – it has always been so:
to wander the cliffs where the sea-breezes blow
and the waves rolling in with the spray flying free
over fathoms of misty-green water below.

I am drawn to the sea – to the sound of the sea:
to the whine of the wind and a wild majesty
in the thunder of waves at the cliff's wetted face,
and the cry of the gulls with their shrill harmony.

I am drawn to the sea – to the slow, rhythmic pace
in the ebb and the flow of continual grace,
while a gathering mist on a grey winter's day
brings the solitude found in this desolate place.

I am drawn to the sea, with the tang of the spray
that lifts from the splintering waves and away...
and away then my thoughts, in the pull and the tow
of swift hidden currents this grave, sombre day.

I am drawn to the sea, where the tides surge and flow
over dark, jagged rocks that gleam brightly below.
Here to wander a while, and to gaze and to know
I am drawn to the sea – it has always been so.

Envelope Stanzas

DUSK

Dusk has come and brings a light rain falling:
a pattering of raindrops on the leaves,
which tremble slightly in a passing breeze
and whisper like a soft voice gently calling.

A time of natural grace that finds me waiting
and sheltering beneath an old oak tree,
whilst out across the fields I chance to see
how cattle stand like statues...hesitating.

The gleam of rain across their wetted shoulders –
reluctant yet to move, content to be
a part of this dim landscape scenery:
as motionless and grey as ancient boulders.

The dark clouds drifting by – a gentle shower
and smell of damp earth rising in the air.
I pause this while with senses made aware
of solitude, and of the passing hour.

A sense of déjà vu, once more recalling
how I have leant against the oak tree's bark
to watch the beauty of the coming dark,
descending like a soft cloak gently falling.

The breeze grows quieter now as if subsiding.
The cattle stir and start to move away
to shelter where the hedgerows slowly sway,
and there to rest unseen where they are hiding.

Bright raindrops, orbs of silver, hang suspended.
The stars will not be seen this cloudy night,
nor meadow softly lit by pale moonlight,
whilst all is hushed and still – the long day ended.

As seen in the previous poem, the envelope stanza provides us with a mirrored rhyme scheme for the four-line stanza:

abba, cddc, and so on

These may be interlinked to give:

abba, bccb, cddc, and so on

Alternatively, we may select a common fourth line rhyme for each stanza, and then arrange combinations of the preceding first three lines:

abax, bcbx, cdcx, and so on.

Paired Stanzas

Another simple format is to combine two 4-line stanzas in matched pairs of rhymes, such as:

abcd, abcd

The result is a poem of 8-line stanzas, but with a subtlety of rhyme, as shown in the following poem.

If we then start to include refrain lines, things can become really interesting:

For example: **abba, bccb, cddc, deed**,

may become: **aBba, BCcb, CDdc, Deed**

In mentioning these options, the intention is not to cause confusion, but simply to demonstrate the way in which stanza forms can be varied to provide various effects.

GREY ON GREY

*Began the day unsettled, yet quite bright –
and I with work to do out in the field.
The grey horizon touched by storms again,
as yet far distant, which might not come near.
And so began the day...though fading light
by later morning seemed to slowly yield
to troubled skies, where thunder clouds of rain
had gathered, and the wind blew loud and clear.*

*So forced to seek protection from the storm
I came into an open barn close by,
while slanting rain fell loud upon the roof
of corrugated iron patched with wood.
And fiercer then came on the thunderstorm
with rising wind across the darkened sky –
and louder, hard upon the metal roof,
the rain drummed down, where sheltered dry I stood.*

*And out across the fields, where pale had been
the winter's morning but a while before,
a darkness came, until the storm passed by
and with the dying wind went peacefully.
Then in the rafters of the barn, unseen,
I heard a pigeon stir and call once more –
and sensing all was well, then saw her fly
out from the barn into a nearby tree.*

*And pausing but a while to sit and preen.
the pigeon then took flight – off and away
across the fields, where distant skies grew clear
and drifting clouds began to show more bright.
So for a while I watched, though faintly seen:
the pigeon slowly fading...grey on grey,
as might a ghost then seem to disappear
before the glimmer of returning light.*

Sapphic Stanza

The sapphic is a classical four-line stanza of non-rhyming lines, and is attributed to the ancient Greek erotic poetess Sappho (625 - 570 BC).

The requirements of this form are concerned solely with the use of meter. The first 3 lines each have five feet (two trochaic then one dactylic followed by two more trochaic), whilst the 4th line has two feet (dactylic and a trochaic). If this is all starting to sound a little too confusing, it may be best shown as follows:

TUM-ti TUM-ti TUM-ti-ty TUM-ti TUM-ti
TUM-ti TUM-ti TUM-ti-ty TUM-ti TUM-ti
TUM-ti TUM-ti TUM-ti-ty TUM-ti TUM-ti
TUM-ti-ty TUM-ti

We know from our previous notes that the trochaic and dactylic forms work well in combination together, to provide a softer (feminine) form to the poem. Given the erotic origin of this stanza form, we might try the following:

SAPPHIC AMBITION

Lost in surging unison – flooding sweetly.
Moaning loudly...constantly... indiscreetly!
Reaching final ecstatic summits neatly –
consumed completely.

Three-Line Stanzas

The three-line stanza is usually referred to as a **triplet** but may sometimes be known as a **terzain**. Various rhyme schemes are possible, and may include simple triple rhymes for each stanza:

aaa bbb ccc .... and so on

Alternatively we may decide on grouping of stanzas into pairs:
abc abc def def
or linked couplets: **aax bbx ccx ddx** .... and so on.

BOOKS IN BOXES

Books in boxes, packed and put away.
Forgotten...almost so, whilst day to day
time passes and our memories decay.

Ornaments and many treasured things
wrapped in newspapers of past happenings,
and lost in boxes, tied with knotted strings.

Glass dishes, pots and pans, and china too –
and cutlery and paintings hid from view
nor yet remembered clearly... this is true.

Life put on hold in bland and rented rooms.
A home in boxes, whilst each day assumes
a drifting where no bright tomorrow blooms.

Books lost in cardboard boxes, plain and grey
with faded labels, waiting for the day
when dusty cobwebs may be brushed away

to rediscover many things once prized.
Old things seen new once more from the disguise
of half-remembered thoughts and bright surprise!

This time of hibernation, that suspends
our present life... yet knowing soon it ends
with treasured books reclaimed like long-lost friends.

A simple triple rhyme in the above poem and in the poem that follows shows how this can be achieved whilst not appearimng too obvious. We see also how enjambment - the unbroken line of one stanza into another, helps also to achieve a steady flow of words.

JERSEY CELEBRATION
(Monterey Hotel, Jersey: 14th August 2007)

The room is rather basic and the bathroom is quite small –
there's a faded print of Jersey harbour hanging on the wall
and a mirror in the wardrobe we can hardly see at all.

The carpet, green and faded, has the usual stains and wear,
with net curtains at the window, which lets in a little air –
and the room so warm and stifling,
though we hardly seem to care.

The sea view we had hoped to find is nowhere to be seen -
it lies far to the south with many rooftops in-between,
and the silhouettes of trees
with their cool shades of summer green.

And the noise of busy traffic, and the sound of hurried feet –
and voices drifting in the breathless calm of summer heat
up to our open window, high above the narrow street.

But the days are warm and sunny, and the sea is bright and blue –
and shaded lanes wind gently as we travel slowly through
to explore this pretty island and discover what is new.

For we have now a few brief days in which to celebrate
your special birthday, honoured with an added token date
of our ultimate retirement, having had so long to wait.

And it matters not the room is small, the lampshade slightly torn:
the bed dipped in the middle and the carpet old and worn –
for this is now the place that sees our new ambition born.

And it matters not of this hotel, or of the rooftop view –
or if the sun is shining and the sky a cloudless blue.
What matters is the days we share and being here with you:

and life and love and happiness, and memories held true
from days to be discovered, and from dreaming old and new.

Several other permutations of rhyme endings are possible when linking three-line stanzas, and in the poem that follows we have a combination of repeated first-line rhymes with couplets:

abb acc add aee ... and so on

ROBBERY

*The crows have come to rob the walnut tree –
perched high on slender branches, where they sway
then swoop and snatch, and quickly fly away.*

*The crows have come – it matters not to me
that they should steal the wrinkled globes of green
in which the ripened walnuts may be seen.*

*Like black rags flapping in the walnut tree
they come and go throughout the autumn day
of late September – up and then away!*

*Away across the field where, placidly,
the idle cattle wander, pause and graze
and gaze beyond these final sunny days.*

*And here am I: witness of robbery,
but not of walnuts or the crows as may
return till all are taken this bright day.*

*The loss I know is of the subtlety
from disappearing leaves of bronze and gold,
and misty mornings of a year grown old.*

*The summer spent: yet bright the memory
of passing seasons, as I pause to see
how crows have come to rob the walnut tree.*

Terza Rima

Terza rima of Italian origin and originally meaning triple rhyme has three-line stanzas, which are arranged to interlink with each other.

This gives us:
> **aba, bcb, cdc, ded** and so on

Terza rima can include as many or as few stanzas as we may wish to have, and is quite flexible in this respect. The lines may also be of any length and in any meter (including the use of mixed meters) which we may decide.

In the poem **"Pebbles"** that follows we see how it is drawn to a conclusion by closing the loop, which refers to the way in which the penultimate line of the poem rhymes with the first line of the start of the poem.

> **aba, bcb, cdc... hah**

Alternatively, we may decide to conclude the poem with a simple triple rhyme stanza as shown in the poem **"Silent Fields"** (page 123):

> **aba, bcb, cdc, ded... jjj**

One other option is to conclude the terza rima with a closing couplet, and if this follows four preceding stanzas, then this neatly provides fourteen lines to become terza rima sonnet:

> **aba, bcb, cdc, ded, ee**

PEBBLES

Petrified like eggs of stone;
revealed by slow receding tide
each frozen pebble waits alone.

One on another, side by side,
they shine beneath the day's bright sky
in gleaming beauty... silent pride.

Recumbent, resting where they lie
exposed to air, becoming dull
as patiently they wait and dry.

Yet warm caress cannot annul
the chilling kiss of sea and sand;
nor yet this brief and measured lull

bring memories to understand
the rough-chipped rock, that once had seen
a fused allegiance to the land.

Too much of time has passed between.
These orbs of stone, worn smooth and round,
no longer speak of what has been.

Surrendering without a sound -
a surly silence marks them free
of alien earth. No longer bound

by any truth, except the sea
that will reclaim them as her own;
and mould their chattering destiny.

SILENT FIELDS

We pause today...pause in our toil,
to view the open countryside
and all that grows in this rich soil.

The silent fields spread far and wide
are quiet now, where once had been
young men who came, and fought and died.

Few signs remain in this fair green,
or tides that wash the nearby shores
of that brave sacrifice once seen.

Few memories of that great cause —
except where monuments now stand
in towns and villages, that pause

with due respect, and close at hand
remember in their silent prayer
those laid to rest in this fair land.

The local names seen listed there
that touch upon each family loss:
a common tragedy they share.

A gentle breeze now blows across
the silent fields: this hallowed ground.
No statue here or holy cross —

no flags that flutter to the sound
of drums and bugles marching by.
No poetry or words profound

in meaning, which might testify
to some great sadness here revealed.
No wreaths beneath a solemn sky

where we, our simple tribute yield.
To pause where all is hushed and stilled
and gaze across a silent field.

Triversan

The triversan is a three line stanza, usually in the form of free verse, having neither rhyme nor meter considerations, but reliant on normal speech. Each stanza, therefore, is a complete sentence, divided into three parts represented by the three lines, where each part is a single phrase. This would follow a natural way of speaking, devoid of any imposed poetical suggestion.

The triversan owes its origin to the native American culture, although this has been developed into its present form by many recent American poets, such as William Carlos Williams (1883 - 1963).

GARDEN TIME

The day begins quite bright and so must I,
for of today there is much planned to do -
despite the distant grey of cloudy sky.

The garden waits – a somewhat daunting view
of tangled grass: in fact, an open field,
although we still deny this to be true.

The garden then, whilst doubtful it may yield
much beauty yet, though daisies come and go
and buttercups with golden flecks revealed.

The dread of toil that waits ahead, we know,
will bring us aches and blisters, whilst such fun
may find us weary as our efforts slow.

Yet grown before the setting of the sun,
a love that flowers there from what is done.

The above poem, whilst in the form of a triversan with an added couplet, also happens to be a terza rima sonnet.

Free verse also works well when presented as three-line stanzas, and these brief stanzas can be mirrored by short lines used to provide a succession of succinct thoughts.

ABSOLUTE NEED

("I write from an absolute inner necessity" - Adrienne Rich)

Not art for art's sake –
nor some inspired thought of nature
seeking to mirror such bright beauty.

Not born of starlight or of fire –
nor the frozen gleam of ice or snow.
on a winter's day.

No sudden vision to inspire some thought –
some secret aim
born of a common need or hidden trust.

Not of some high ambition
that I might seek, as best I might,
this coin of rhyme and meter.

Only a voice that whispers
of an absolute need and necessity
to drive the need, whereby I write.

Five-Line Stanzas

Five-line stanzas offer a variety of rhyme schemes. For example, they may be sometimes made from the simple ballad form: **abab** with an added rhyming line to give a couplet to each stanza: **ababb**

WORRY A LITTLE, IF YOU MUST

Worry about me if you must
for I am small and in need of care,
and you are all that I know and trust.
My whole world we together share –
ever with me... ever there.

Worry a while, from time to time,
if I do not sleep or appear unwell –
or if my nature seems out of rhyme
with our happy days, and seems to dwell
upon some passing colic spell.

Worry... but do not worry too much,
for I grow strong and have learnt to trust
in all you do and your gentle touch.
Learn, as you will, to relax and adjust
yet worry a little...if you must.

We may even simply combine a three-line stanza of one rhyme ending with a couplet of another: **aaabb**

Another arrangement might be place a couplet within the stanza:
abaab

Clearly the number of possible combinations are many, although there is a need, having adopted a particular pattern, to maintain this throughout the poem.

One other simple form of the five-line stanza is to have a refrain line at the end of each stanza, or perhaps at the start of stanzas as shown by the following poem:
Abcbc Adede Afgfg ...and so on

FIVE-ACRE FIELD

The farmer and the farmer's wife
walk out across five-acre field.
The breathless air is stilled and warm,
though distant clouds may yield a storm
that starts to build.

The farmer and the farmer's wife,
with time enough to come and see
an amber sea of corn that sways
and ripples in the distant haze
of autumn days.

The farmer and the farmer's wife
who talk together, walking slow
and passing by the hedgerow where
wild summer flowers come and go,
remembered there.

The farmer and the farmer's wife
who smile, recalling long ago
how they had spent a summer's day
when hidden in the hay they lay
in love and play.

The farmer and the farmer's wife
with warm, contented days that build
this life they know: the rich earth tilled
and seeds sown in five-acre field
that slowly grow

Slightly less obvious arrangements may be achieved through the matching of stanzas, and possibly the repetition of particular words. For example:
AeBee CgDgg AmBmm CoDoo ArBrr CsDss

In the poem that follows, lines **A,B.C** and **D** are not true refrain lines, but do have the same word endings which tend to provide a subtle echo through the poem.

JOURNEY ONWARD

*I make no sense of this long journey,
which began so long ago,
long before my understanding –
knowing I might never know
how it is I travel so.*

*From the distance, I remember
days once spent in childhood play,
though I travelled...travelled forward
always moving on my way –
woken to another day.*

*Others also on my journey
taught of what they thought they knew,
adding to my understanding
though, in truth, there were but few
who glimpsed the far horizon view.*

*Little more can I remember
of the few who taught me so,
as I journeyed slowly forward
from a time of long ago –
learning what I had to know.*

*Onward then, my constant journey
brought a time when I might play
a part within my understanding:
self-reliant, face the day
and with a choice to find my way.*

*This then all I now remember,
though the future days grow few
upon my journey further forward.
To pause..to sleep, perhaps to view
a reason for the days I knew.*

Six-Line Stanzas

The six-line stanza (**sestet**) offers even more permutations and combinations than those we have already seen. Indeed, we could follow this statement with several pages of examples, but for now will confine ourselves to just a few.
For example:
          ababab cdcdcd ...and so on

A WINTER'S DAY

A haloed moon portends tomorrow's rain -
sweet benediction on a dormant earth
grown barren in the autumn chill again.
Omens of winter... this, an idle mirth,
that haunts the silvered eventide domain
of meted time with memory of birth.

Bright orbs of jet, the honeysuckled fruits
of second flowering echo sweet recall
of summer's scarlet globes, and spent pursuits
from heady fragrance bonded in the thrall
of damp and musty odours, where deep roots
rest shrouded dark beneath a leaf-strewn pall.

Unique, white-throated blackbird, busy now –
wise witness of two graceful summers seen.
Auger of conjured fates that may endow
some quiet expectation and a keen
yet ill-conceived awareness, with the vow
and promises of season's change foreseen.

Metallic dawn with bright and chilly gleam.
The iron grey of sombre, rain-filled skies
reflected in a slow, lethargic stream
that sadly echoes winter's weary sighs.
Anaemic day: this hushed and passive theme
of dull hours drifting by that symbolise
a time of rest... a gentle, haunting dream
of hope and memory...and spring sunrise.

Whilst not wanting to make things too obvious, it is a nice touch to think that some subtle arrangement of rhyme ending can at least be seen by the more discerning reader!

For example:
abcabc defdef ...and so on

A RUSTED HOOK

A simple thing...a rusted hook,
like an inverted question mark
forgotten in the old oak beam.
Scarce noticed till I chanced to look
where remnants of a peeling bark
reveal the hardened, wooden seam.

A rusted hook...its ancient charm
part-hidden in the shadowed cleft
of roof and wall, hung in the days
once known, when the abandoned farm
held life and purpose, long-since left
to memories of ancient ways.

And floating in the dusty air
a hush now fills the empty space,
where errant breezes swirl and die.
Like ghosts, it seems, suspended there –
lost in a time that haunts this place,
and sees the days go drifting by.

Sesta Rima

The sesta rima is a particular form of the six-line stanza, which effectively includes a quatrain combined with couplet rhymes.

The rhyme scheme becomes: **ababcc**.

The traditional sesta rima is written in iambic meter with alternate lengths of pentameter (5 feet) and tetrameter (4 feet). Modern versions may allow a degree of flexibility applied to the length of the lines.

This stanza arrangement was much favoured by William Shakespeare (1564 - 1616), and is sometimes referred to as the **"Venus and Adonis"** stanza in recognition of his narrative poem of the same name. The final couplet can also be used to provide an emphasised effect to each stanza, as shown in the poem that follows:

> *HOW SO?*
>
> *If from this friendship we have come to know,*
> *how might it be we rise above*
> *our hum-drum, stumbling steps, with hearts aglow?*
> *How might it be, we then find love?*
> *How then that from such dreams we come to see*
> *and touch upon our destiny?*
>
> *If given time for words of gentle grace,*
> *these are expressed in poetry –*
> *though lightly written, should the days erase*
> *or likewise fade from what might be?*
> *How might it be, though love may dwell unsure,*
> *that we, together, search for more?*

Seven-Line Stanzas

A stanza or poem of seven lines is known generally as a **septet**. These are sometimes formed from the addition of a single refrain line to the standard sestet, with this refrain included for all stanzas.

For example:
                abcabcX defdefX ...and so on

Other septets with all manner of rhyme endings are possible, but as previously observed, simpler arrangements tend to work best.

For example:
                ababbba cdcdddc

LUNACY

From the east...the mysterious east, she came,
in gossamer veils of silver and white.
Her beauty hidden, yet of such fame
that sad men lingered in shades of night –
tormented and waiting, to catch but a sight
of her passing by in a sea of light...
to watch and to whisper again her name.

And onward...westward, her passing by
in a realm of magical mystery,
and shrouded by a cloudy sky.
Hidden from those who had hoped to see
as she came and went, unseen and free....
like the ever-turning tides of the sea
and the haunting scream of a seagull's cry.

Rhyme Royal

The rhyme royal is a particular form of septet stanza, and has a rhyme scheme of
> **ababbcc**

It is written in an iambic meter, although any number of feet is quite normal.

DAYS THAT PASS

The days pass by... our routine set in place
to fill the hours, though little more than this –
and rarely now a time when we embrace
or reason find to share a tender kiss.
Worse yet, as something we no longer miss:
of no more meaning than a fading rhyme,
as if we never knew of such a time

Sometimes a smile...sometimes a tender word,
when sat together, briefly, face to face.
A memory, perhaps, of things once heard:
a love once known, of which we find no trace
from days that pass with routine set in place.
An idle conversation we may share,
spoken by lovers, who no longer care.

The rhyme royal may be a complete poem in itself, or might be written as a stanza in a longer poem. One particular arrangement of rhyme royal stanzas will be found in a traditional form of poetry known as the ballade royal, where the last line of each stanza is written as a refrain line.

We will look at this and other traditional forms of poetry later, but may note in passing how the selection of a particular stanza can have a significant effect on the final poem. Finding the required subtle rhymes can provide something of a challenge too!

The Ottava Rima

It is apparent from the name that we have moved up into eight-line stanzas of Italian origin, although the rhyme scheme suggests that all we have done, effectively, is to extend the sesta rima stanza by two middle lines.
This gives us the rhyme scheme: **abababcc**

UNIMPORTANT THINGS

*I have learnt my lessons well –
of how we find in little things
where the brightest memories dwell.
Unimportant happenings
that come to hold a magic spell
and secret charm, which true love brings.
Little things that seem to count
and build into a large amount.*

*Little things: a smile, a kiss –
to walk together, hand in hand.
These are the moments we might miss,
not found in grander things, nor planned.
And well then to remember this –
how, given time, we understand
the simple truth of which I tell,
from having learnt my lessons well.*

The Sicilian Octave

Another eight-line stanza is the Sicilian octave, with what appears to be a deceptively simple construction of:

abababab

The difficulty of such a stanza form is in trying to avoid the "sledge-hammer" effect of obvious rhymes when repeated so often in each stanza.

The Eight-Line Stanza

It is obvious that an eight-line stanza might have any combination of rhyme endings. As we have already seen, many eight-line stanzas may come about simply through the combination of two four-line (ballad) stanzas. I will leave this for you to discover and experiment with as you may.

However, there is one recognised form known as <u>the</u> eight-line stanza which has a rhyme scheme:

ababbcbc

AS BEFORE

I come again to where we met
and all is as it was before,
though it may be that I forget
some things of which I am not sure.
The trees seem taller, maybe more,
yet still the pathway wanders through
where sparrows come that sing and soar,
like those same birds, which once we knew.

And there...the same old fallen tree
where once we sat, and passing came
the happy days you spent with me
one summer, with a burning flame.
Though strange it is to speak your name –
as if to call you here with me,
when all appears to be the same
yet is not so, nor cannot be.

We may readily see this as being the easy combination of two simple four-line stanzas **(abab, bcbc)**. However, this particular stanza is used when writing a traditional form of poetry, known simply as the eight-line stanza ballade.

It is enough, for now, to know that at least one stanza of eight lines exists in recognized traditional form, although there are many others as we will come to discover later.

Triolet

The triolet dates back to early 13th century medieval French poetry, with a distinctive use of refrain lines. The triolet has eight lines and the slightly misleading name (which might imply a triple form of some kind) actually refers to the use of a triple refrain line.

ABaAabAB

As we have already seen, refrain lines can be useful in underlining some aspect or meaning of the poem. However, when used in the brief single stanza format of the triolet, they should (wherever possible) try to blend into the flow of words, and appear more subtle.

The traditional format for the triolet is in iambic tetrameter (4 feet), but modern variations are known.

TRUTH UNSPOKEN

Much of truth remains unspoken –
virtue needs no strident voice.
Truth remains, though words be broken...
much of truth remains unspoken.
Words are but the merest token
of an honest, silent choice.
Much of truth remains unspoken –
virtue needs no strident voice.

The triolet is frequently a single stanza poem, and we will see this again later when we come to consider various poem structures.

HERE WITH ME

What better place to be
than here, and you with me.
The days we share and see -
what better place to be
in love, contentedly.
This harmony... this destiny:
what better place to be
than have you here with me.

The Spenserian Stanza

The Spenserian stanza invented by the Elizabethan poet Edmund Spenser (1552 - 1599) is an unusual stanza form of nine lines, with a mixed rhyme pattern, which serves well to disguise any obviousness. In fact, we may readily recognise this as being the traditional eight-line stanza ballade

ababbcbc

with an added line to provide a final couplet:

Therefore we have: **ababbcbcc**

The Spenserian stanza is usually written in an iambic pentameter (5 feet) for the first eight lines and an iambic hexameter (6 feet) for the ninth line.

The iambic hexameter (6 feet) owes its origin to ancient Greek poetry and is known as an Alexandrine.

SPENCER RHYME

The Spenser stanza has a steady pace
of bold iambic meter clearly seen,
although (perhaps) a tendency to race -
a flood of words, with scarce a pause between.

Yet onwards then, for this has always been
a cadence found in words that brightly chime.
A forward rush on five feet builds this screen
of hurried phrases, set to measured rhyme...
but not the Alexandrine, which will take its time.

A more modern and liberal interpretation of the Spenserian stanza may allow a change of meter and number of feet, although the rhyme scheme is retained.

FIRESIDE THOUGHTS

The ending of another busy day,
when we may sit together by the fire
and talk of many things that came our way,
and of ambitions, which our dreams inspire.
Contented then, with all that we desire
from simple things – the log fire's gentle blaze
and warmth of love to fill the heart's desire.
What need of more – except to sit and gaze,
nor seek to change the measure of our autumn days.

The Wren Stanza

It may seem a little arrogant to claim some particular stanza form as original, since there will inevitably be an example lurking somewhere, written many years before. However, if only to establish having resurrected such a possible stanza, I will here give mention of the Wren stanza, which has a rhyme scheme:

abcbacbca

This was originally derived from a gathering of three triple rhymes with compositions of (**abc bac bca**). The attraction of this arrangement is that each stanza has three triple rhymes, but separated in a manner that helps to disguise any obviousness of rhyme.

IF FAME BE OURS

*If we achieve as much as we might do -
and gladly so, if such has been our aim
to do, as best we might, such things and more.
If there are those who know, and speak our name,
to tell of our achievements, though but few,
and brief our footprints on this honoured shore.
For all must pass, as will the cloak of fame,
which others wore – to pass on as before,
whilst we, forgotten, know this to be true.*

The Ten-Line Stanza

Clearly it is possible to have any number of lines in a stanza, but we will mention the ten-line stanza, since it will be seen later as the stanza form found in the ballade supreme (see page 172).

The rhyme scheme becomes:

ababbccdcd

Why the rhyme scheme should be so is not known, but may have originated from the combination of two four-line ballad stanzas (**abab** and **cdcd**) with a simple (**bc**) link, giving two middle couplets.

abab + bc + cdcd

KNOWING NOW

*I would like to know now, at the time of my going –
of the journey ahead for which I am preparing,
as to what destination will fate be bestowing?
Whilst declaring (at this early stage little caring)
what direction I take – not despairing nor swearing
of some cursed, unrehearsed few more days left to borrow.
Far beyond all the woe-ing and slowing and sorrow...
all the heaving of bosoms, bereaving and grieving –
I would like to know now what will happen tomorrow,
so I can prepare for my ultimate leaving.*

Other Classical Forms

Several other classical stanza forms exist, many of which date back to medieval French poetry, and are often recognised by the repetition of refrain lines. Refrain lines are usually derived from the first lines of the poems, and may include the complete first lines or a phrase, or even a single word.

Such poems including rondels, rondeaus, roundels, rondelets, and roundelays, are described in a separate section (see page 173), together with rules concerning their construction. The roundelay in particular has a relaxed construction with a loose and less restrictive format, which allows the required repetition of refrain lines to occur at any position in the poem, as shown by the following examples.

NEVER MINE

The words I write are never mine:
they come... a whisper in the night,
which then reveals each gifted line
and brings a sudden, new delight.

Clear phrases found that seem to shine
from some dark source, and then take flight.
The words I write are never mine.

Each poem of unique design -
and though they gleam so clear and bright,
the words I write are never mine.

Some slight disguising of the refrain lines is also possible in the division and presentation of lines and stanzas, as shown below.

WORDS REMAINING HERE

These thoughts on paper: words remaining here
in lines of rhyme that show a part of me -
although quite how or why is never clear.

This measurement of dreams that cannot be,
yet dwell unseen and seem to linger near
in sentences, by which I come to see
these thoughts on paper.

Words remaining here
in poems, which as suddenly appear -
like whispered words I struggle to set free.
These thoughts on paper ...words remaining here

The Sonnet

A final mention, perhaps, of the sonnet, which is required always to have fourteen lines to provide the complete poem. Longer poems may, of course, have more than one sonnet stanza. Many rhyme schemes are possible, most of which tend to follow a construction made up from the subtle sub-division of two quatrains and a sestet.

For example:
Shakespearean (English) sonnet	**abab cdcd efef gg**
Petrarchian (Italian) sonnet	**abba abba cde cde**
Spencer sonnet	**abab bcbc cdcd ee**
Terza Rima sonnet	**aba bcb cdc ded ee**

These divisions are not always obvious since the sonnet tends to be written as a single stanza. We will look at these variations in more detail later, but sufficient for now to note that there are many types, each of which has some unique form of construction and rhyme sequence. There is clearly more to the sonnet than the simple counting of lines.

THE POET'S GIFT

I have not much to give, yet I have this
the gift of words: a poet's easy charm.
A gathering of thoughts, as if to kiss
my one true love, whom they seek to disarm.
This then my gift of an ethereal grace:
a whisper fading softly in the air,
or cyphered words, by which I seek to place
a token of the harmony we share.

Yet more than this, as is the poet's skill
to touch the heart and gently linger there.
Though days drift on, yet will this gift fulfil
the constant charm of true love made aware.

Nor gold, nor silver gifts bring more delight –
nor diamond ever shine more true and bright.

The sonnet is also traditionally written in iambic pentameter (5 feet) but in more modern versions we can vary this to include different meters and/or longer lengths.

Mixed Lengths of Stanzas

Having looked at so many stanzas with fixed numbers of lines and rhyme schemes, many of which are necessary when writing traditional forms of poetry, it is (perhaps) as well to remind ourselves that all rules are made to be broken...if necessary. The essential requirement at all times will be to ensure that the poem is set down in a way that satisfies the poet and, ultimately, the reader.

AUGURED GRACES

Ambition is the ascending song
of the lonesome lark,
or the sudden throng
of sparrows in the old oak tree –
the boisterous, shrill cacophony
of territorial dispute.

Hope is the long, uncertain route
of mass migration seeking still
some respite from grey, winter's chill.
Hope is a journey through the night
that seeks the warmth of morning light.

Faith is the courage to remain –
the robin's frosted bright domain
of silver grace... the bitter chill
that measures days of iron will.

Faith is the nightingale that sings,
and with such sudden music brings
a beauty to the empty park:
a lone voice calling in the dark.

TRADITIONAL POETRY

Sonnets

Having looked at various stanzas and their construction, we may now consider where and when these appear in many traditional forms of poetry. It would seem reasonable to begin our study of traditional forms with the sonnet, which is (perhaps) one of the best-known of all forms of poetry.

The term "sonnet" derives from the Italian for "little song", which is where this form of poetry originated. It is said to have been first used by Giaromo da Lentini, a 13th century Italian poet, in correspondence with other poets. Traditionally, a sonnet will have fourteen lines with each line in iambic pentameter. This form has endured for centuries and seems likely to remain so, although some slight degree of latitude is sometimes seen in more modern sonnets, through a relaxation of meter or length of lines.

Consider, for example the following Shakespearean sonnet:

DUMB BEASTS

Dumb beasts are they, born of a stupid guile,
which know of nothing but a field of grass
in which to graze, contented all the while
to see the days and changing seasons pass.

Dim-witted, of a dull and witless sense,
with scarce awareness of the sun and rain.
Their world constrained by an electric fence –
devoid of all emotion to explain

how sometimes, of no reason, they may run
or rub their heads together when they feed.
How can it be that they might know of fun
or pleasures found, that serve no basic need?

Dumb beasts – mere cattle, ignorant of care
and of a nature we may never share.

It is hardly surprising to discover that there are several types of sonnet, many of which are named after poets, whose frequent and adept use helped to established them. Before looking at these many variations, let us first remind ourselves of a few "rules", which may not always be very obvious.

The sonnet on the previous page has lines in the traditional iambic pentameter (5 feet), and although appearing to be simply a poem of fourteen lines, it is slightly more complicated than this and includes subtle divisions. A sonnet requires the introduction of an initial theme or a proposal, which is then considered or developed in some way, leading to a final satisfying conclusion - often expressed in a succinct couplet.

Most sonnets follow this traditional arrangement, which may be shown by their appearance with spaces between groups of lines, although this is often thought to be neither necessary nor desirable. The sonnet is more frequently seen as a single stanza poem.

In other instances, this division of proposal and assessment may be further emphasised by the rhyme scheme, which will also vary for particular types of sonnets.

Shakespearean or English Sonnet

The English sonnet was actually in popular use by many famous poets at the time, and came to be known later as the Shakespearean sonnet out of respect and recognition of so gifted a writer.

The Shakespearean sonnet has three quatrains and a couplet. The first two quatrains introduce the subject and the third quatrain then contemplates or develops this in some way, before the concluding couplet draws the poem to a close.

The rhyme scheme for the Shakespearean sonnet is quite straightforward:

abab cdcd efef gg

Sometimes this is enhanced through repeated rhyme, which may draw upon any combination and permutation of rhymes...too many to even start to list, but for example:

> **abab acac adad aa**
> **abab acac bcbc dd**

At all times, however, the final couplet is very much a "stand-alone" aspect of the poem, bringing with it a very sharp and succinct observation. There are many examples where this final couplet has become so well remembered, that it has been absorbed into the English language as some wise adage or saying.

MOVING ON

The final box is packed and has been taken —
possessions safely wrapped and put away
like memories, that briefly we awaken
and keep protected from the light of day.
Lost, dusty treasures found in attic spaces
from long-forgotten years we hid from view.
Small tokens kept of dim and distant places,
we carry with us now to somewhere new.

The past we cling to: habits and traditions
that lend a present meaning to our lives.
Abandoned aims replaced with bright ambitions,
to bring a hope reborn from what survives.

What then of new dreams we may later find?
What ghosts in empty rooms we leave behind?

In the above example we see that the rule regarding lines of the iambic pentameter has been broken.. or slightly bent anyway! A softer rhyme ending has been introduced on many of the lines by means of an added unstressed syllable, which slows the poem slightly and allows us to linger over what is being said.

We are reminded of the fact that rules may be regarded as flexible when there is an intentional desire to add to the poem in some way. In most cases the use of an iambic meter will prevail, although as we have already seen, longer line lengths are also possible. Modern versions of the sonnet may, for example, may be extended to include lines of iambic heptameter, as shown in the poem that follows:

NASTURTIUMS

A sunny week has barely passed since scattered seeds were sown
along the garden wall – there, in the dark-brown, fertile ground.
And yet, already risen, small amoeba leaves have grown,
with promise soon of coloured trumpet flowers all around.

And comes a thought of childhood and nasturtiums I once grew -
and schooldays then recalled with many tutors, long ago.
And Mr Beckensale – he, one of many, who I knew
that taught us English grammar... which he said we ought to know.

And of his love of poetry...though alien then to me:
his dreary lessons passing with each long, slow, weary hour.
The scattered seeds on stony ground, that he might never see
some small, green leaf or, given time, that first bright, fragile flower.

And might have read this poem, quite amazed...and softly smiled
to find himself remembered by so difficult a child.

The sonnet may also encompass many moods, assisted by a variation in meter away from the traditional iambic pentameter. The use of mixed meter can give the poem a contemporary feel, matching the frank honesty of other emotions, as shown in the poem that follows:

LOVERS WE WERE

Lovers we were, true lovers long after
the dreams of an idyllic love when we started.
Lovers with passion and lusting and laughter,
long after the pretence of romance departed.

The silk and the lace of each ardent seduction –
insatiable gratification then born
from our naked awareness and tender instruction:
the heat of the night and the chill of the dawn.

A simple arrangement, uncluttered by dreaming
and lacking endearments to muddle the mind.
No poems or roses or other gifts, seeming
to hint at some aesthetic grace we might find.

Just an honesty shared and a time of desire,
with a lingering warmth we enjoyed from that fire.

Petrarchian or Italian Sonnet

The Petrarchian sonnet originated with the Italian poet Guittone d'Arezzo (1235 - 1294) and was later popularised by Francesco Petrarch (1304 - 1374). It was introduced into England by Sir Thomas Wyatt (1503 - 1542) during the early 16th century.

Its construction has two quatrains that set the theme and a sestet to provide a conclusion to the poem. Both quatrains have the same rhymes, whilst the sestet may be more properly described as two tercets, although combined into a unified summary.

The rhyme scheme is then: **abba abba cde cde**

Traditionally, a break is usually made between the octet and sestet, to emphasise their significance.

SONNET OF SILVER FIRE

What then this art that Petrarch did embrace?
What beauty stirred and heard in words benign.
of metric wit, the written scripts define?
What chart ...what sparkled path of charm and grace?
What then this tryst, which time and rhyme might place
in hidden depths of deft, expressive line?
What strict, yet rhythmic rhetoric design,
occurring with unerring pace and grace?

Behold – it is of bold iambus born:
of regimented, pentametric class,
and yet rhymes silhouette sets this desire.
Discreetly then, the secret to adorn –
as in completion of Venetian glass:
the honest sonnet skilled with silver fire.

Spenser Sonnet

Edmund Spenser (1552-1599) developed a sonnet form based on his fascination with interlocking rhymes. We have already seen an example of this in the Spenserian stanza:

ababbcbcc

Similarly then, the Spenser sonnet has three quatrains and a couplet and we may note again the use of a strong rhyming couplet to bring the poem to a sharp conclusion:

abab bcbc cdcd ee.

LOVES MANY SHARED

*Loves many that we share: the one
held manifest in this delight
of words that come from thoughts begun
upon a bold, uncertain flight.*

*Each new adventure held in sight
is with ambition bravely run:
whilst inspiration and a bright
imagination sees it done.*

*This wandering through ideas spun
from literary aims, which might
explore new ways: new phrases won
like wonders lit by candle-light.*

*Loves many that we share – such fun
here found in you, my dearest son.*

Other Sonnets

We will not be surprised to learn that many poets throughout the ages have come to discover the sonnet and have experimented with the requirement of fourteen lines in a manner to make it their own. For some poets this has come to be almost an obsession, to the exclusion of all other ways of writing poetry.

Milton Sonnet

Modern sonnets tend to be presented as a single stanza, and in the case of the Petrarchian sonnet, when written in this manner, it is more commonly referred to as a Milton sonnet after John Milton (1608 - 1674).

The rhyme scheme is then: **abbaabbacdecde**

Wilfred Owen

If we look at more recent poets, such as Wilfred Owen (1893 - 1918) and his famous poem "Anthem for Doomed Youth", we discover his sonnet is presented as two stanzas with the rhyme scheme:

abab cdcd / effe gg

Modern Sonnets

Modern sonnets may employ all manner of variations, such as the example that follows, which has a rhyme scheme:

abc abc def def gg

JANUARY

This lunar midnight of silver and black
with scattered stars in a velvet void:
this profound awareness of space and time.

This lingering silence and looking back
over past achievements, with thoughts deployed
in the crafted words of meter and rhyme.

Another new year and another new dream:
the challenge once more of another dawn
and all that lingers, as yet unknown.

Like frosted fields that sparkle and gleam
in a hushed pause, waiting the new day drawn
beneath winter skies, and this time alone.

A time to build on ambition once more
for the onward journey... on as before.

Gerard Manley Hopkins

Gerard Manley Hopkins (1844 - 1889) was noted for writing almost all of his poems his own preferred sonnet form, presented as two stanzas:

abba abba / cdc dcd

As previously mentioned he was unique amongst poets in his use of "sprung verse". In order to emphasise this effect he included accents where changes in emphasis or pauses were required. This tended to distort words from their normal pronunciation, but achieved measured stresses along the lines, which was his clear intention. The full effect of this is probably best experienced by reading his poetry aloud.

He also used a great deal of assonance and alliteration, which added to the "chiming" effect and general harmony of his poetry. The poem that follows is my own attempt at this "challenging" form. Irregular, stressed vowels are indicated by accents above the letters concerned.

EVERLONG

It is a dawn-day drawn made morning of the lone lark
rousèd arisen-raised up, upward upon a thread of song,
whilst sparrows of a squabble-scramble bright along
their leafy realm, sea-shade shadowèd-green and dark.
Aloft of ancient antlers, broadèn-branch and bark
rough agèd, grey-hung, swung a-swinging off along
o'er ancient trunks ringèd of seasons, stirred and strong
astride the lane — field, fallow yield:
                      the buildèd hedgerows mark.

Continuèd of ways, days dull tradition rooted as must trees
stand sentinel to ownership, markèd fixed and view,
time-wrought, bought, fought-for: taught of boundaries,
as, likewise, recognised of prizèd knowledge new.
Schooled wise in this consistency, safe-certain seize
upon such knowledge, ever-once and everlong held true.

Gerard Manley Hopkins also devised what he called the **Curtal Sonnet**, although this was not what we would consider to be a sonnet in the accepted sense, since it had only eleven lines. For this reason we shall come to look at this form later (see page 184).

Terza Rima Sonnet

When looking at stanza forms we had considered the terza rima with its linking of three lines. If four such stanzas are written with a final couplet, this will provide us with a unique form of sonnet:

aba bcb cdc ded ee

AUTUMN NOW

Autumn now: a time of gathered leaves
with tangled branches trimmed and cut away –
made tidy from the sculpture this achieves.

A busy time throughout the passing day –
with wood and twigs and coloured leaves piled high:
the musty scent of nature and decay.

Beneath a dull and dappled cloudy sky,
smoke rising from the bonfire's drifting haze
with sudden sparks that burst and upwards fly.

Autumn now: the ending of the days
in ruins of a summertime stripped bare –
with all of loss and sadness this portrays.

Tools cleaned and put away, whilst made aware
how winter's chill now lingers in the air.

The construction of most sonnets suggests that the first eight lines introduce an initial theme and the remaining six lines then provide an assessment and conclusion. However, with the terza rima form of three-line stanzas, this may allow the development of a theme over three tercets (nine lines) with a concluding tercet and a final couplet.

These finer aspects of the sonnet may often be missed when the poem is read, but will influence the feel of a well-rounded poem.

WHERE SHADOWS GROW

I wonder, sometimes, where my memories go?
Not far, I think, for sometimes they return
reminding me of what I used to know.

There are so many things I may still learn.
The list goes on and on – not finished yet,
whilst other facts then disappear in turn.

Though mostly I forget what I forget:
this one slim benefit I seem to find
by way of payment for an unknown debt.

And trailing my forgotten past behind,
I look to see what more I need to know.
What new discovery to fill my mind
but for a while: a brief and warming glow.
A flame that flickers, where the shadows grow.

Wren Sonnet

There is nothing to prevent us from devising our own form of sonnet, possibly repeating something done before of which we are blissfully unaware. By way of example, the Wren sonnet is an acrostic poem with the rhyme scheme:
abba cddc eff eaa

A NEW WREN SONNET

Ambition serves a hope that I might write
New words...some new arrangement, which will reach
Each nuance of expression found in speech.
Words that will be selected, clear and bright,
With honesty to bring my thoughts alive...
Rebuild achievement of this written art.
Each brave adventure then, which sees the start –
Nor doubts how, given time, I will revive
Some bright discovery and thereby learn
Of journeys made, where I have never been.
New paths that pass beyond old language seen:
New words that flow like streams, and give in turn
Each poem greater depth...and yet take flight
To sparkle brightly in the morning light.

Bending The Rules

Clearly a modern sonnet may seek to "bend the rules" slightly, whilst maintaining the fourteen lines required.

As we have seen, such changes may indeed be quite subtle and include variations in meter or length of lines, which depart from the traditional iambic pentameter (5 feet). Traditional and modern variations in new or recognised rhyme schemes may add further to the presentation and diversity of the sonnet.

By way of example the following sonnet, **"A Gathering Of Dreams"**, is written in a paeon meter (ti-**TUM**-ti-ty) with iambic meter (ti-**TUM**) line endings. This mixing of meters is then combined into a form of simple rhyming couplets.

By comparison, the sonnet **"Reflections By A Pond"**, whilst appearing to adhere to the strict iambic pentameter discipline, would seem stilted if read aloud in this way, and consequently requires a more natural form of expression.

A GATHERING OF DREAMS

I write this for the memory of those we will not share -
of all the many things you did when I was never there.
Things great and small... the many and the very special few,
which linger always in your thoughts: the ones I never knew.

I write this for the days...the golden seasons that passed by
when I could not be there beside you, and the reasons why.
The distances dividing us, that held us far apart -
yet ever in my thoughts with you, and ever in my heart.

I write this for the memory of words we never said -
that echo in the void of lonely days that wait ahead.
The letters that I meant to write and things I meant to say,
drifting in forgotten mists until they fade away.

A gathering of dreams we might have shared... yet not to be,
and these few words upon a page that you will never see.

REFLECTIONS BY A POND

What is it that you see reflected there
beside the pond, in waters cool and deep -
while mirrored clouds drift by, as if aware
of that calm realm where dreaming goldfish sleep?

What calm and gentle thoughts, or idle dreams
float gently in that soft, green-shadowed gloom
of cloud water, where the sunlight gleams
and pure and white the water lilies bloom?

What beauty then revealed... what time of ease
sat for a while beside the limpid pool?
What whispering of secrets in the trees,
where summer breezes come, so hushed and cool?

What bright reflections there for you to see,
of memories or dreams of what may be?

Quatorzain

The quatorzain is the name given to any irregular form of sonnet. This modern form will invariably have as part of its construction the use of a random rhyme arrangement, which may include loosely spaced couplets or several lines of the same rhyme ending, again at irregular intervals in the poem.

This relaxed style of rhyme is often found in modern poetry, and likewise helps disguise any obviousness or predictability normally seen in the sonnet construction, as shown by the following example:

QUATORZAIN

The quatorzain appears to bend the rules
of what a normal sonnet ought to be –
and seems to wander on quite aimlessly,
which really is not what we would expect.

The rhymes (and there are rhymes), fall here and there
as if by chance – like secret, hidden jewels,
although in time we slowly might detect
a pattern, which (though difficult to see)
is equally as awkward to ignore.

The quatorzain is seen as poetry
of modern form, and likewise due respect –
for what is new today may lead to more,
and give to us a greater gift to share
of which we are not certain or aware.

Sonnet Sequence

Some epic poems are made from sonnet stanzas, and are referred to as a sonnet sequence. Any number of sonnet stanzas may be used, and may be combined in various ways for added effect, such as the use of refrain lines.

Sonnet sequences are also known where one poet writes the first poem and passes this to another poet, who adds a second sonnet before passing it to another poet.... and so on. One can only imagine what length this sequence might attain, or indeed what direction such an accumulation of thoughts and ideas may lead, and will probably be of some surprise when finally returned to the originator.

Sonnet of Sonnets

One other form of sonnet sequence is found in a sonnet of sonnets. This is a somewhat lengthy poem of 210 lines, which begins by writing an introduction sonnet. Each line of this initial sonnet is then taken in turn as the first line for the fourteen sonnets that follow.

From experience I can only advise that an attempt to write what is an epic poem should not be undertaken lightly. Once started, it becomes a work of dedication. I have resisted any temptation to include such a poem in this book, since this would increase the size greatly and be of dubious additional benefit.

Summary

Whilst the sonnet is very much a traditional form of poetry, we have seen how it may be readily changed to reflect modern trends. The requirement for fourteen lines is sacrosanct, but "rules" concerning rhyme and meter offer a great deal of freedom and experimentation.

The final example that follows has an irregular meter, allowing necessary pauses as if to hesitate and reflect on what is being said.

VIDI FINEM BELLI MORTUOS

"Only the dead have seen an end to war" - Plato

Only the dead have seen an end to war,
who know of endless sleep, nor stir from rest
in vain pursuit of all that went before.

Only the dead, who may all hope invest
in some unknown ambition left to save,
beyond all futile prayers and last request.

Yet none may know what waits beyond the grave
in that black chasm where all souls must dwell -
if any such survive in that dark cave.

Only the dead, who can no longer tell
of any truth beyond that final door,
or of what may be found in heaven or hell.

At peace... at rest upon some distant shore,
only the dead have seen an end to war.

Ballads and Ballades

Early History

At a time when minstrels travelled the land, telling of great kings, mighty battles, epic heroes and lovely maidens, and perhaps an occasional dragon, the stories they brought with them were sung as ballads. These were often traditional tunes, to which they could add their own words.

Many of the ballads were of simple construction but would include refrain lines, intended to reinforce some aspect of the celebrated tale and often to encourage the audience to join in with a rousing chorus.

SINGS THE ROBIN

Sings the robin, this bright morning
with a constant, cheerful song –
watching from his leafy awning
as I work my way along

the garden plot...the rich soil turning
to the rhythm of the spade,
till of some brief respite earning
seek I then a welcome shade.

Sings the robin, pausing briefly
to inspect the measured worth
of my labours there, though chiefly
seeking worms there in damp earth.

Watching him as he watched me,
while idle moments drift away:
then to my digging cheerfully
whilst sings the robin this bright day.

So it was that the ballad became a recognised form of poetry set to music – the pop music of its day. Indeed, the notion of modern music is seen to have evolved directly from this self-same tradition.

Fortunately, at some time in the past, when people began to achieve literacy, someone decided to write down the more widely known ballads and ballades of the time, before they faded from memory.

The notion of writing ballads and ballades persisted, from which early written poetry evolved. There were rules, of course, by which poems would be written in various forms.

The ballade was of French origin whilst fulfilling the same task as the English ballad. It may seem pedantic to talk of ballads and ballades, but they were of different derivations and, as we shall see, follow quite different forms of construction.

The Ballad

The ballad has four-line stanzas, where the 2nd and 4th lines always rhyme. Very often the 1st and 3rd lines also rhyme, so that the ballad construction (**abab**) is what many of us come to think of as "normal" poetry. The use of internal rhyme is also included sometimes but is optional.

The stanzas are of simple construction and written in iambic meter, with alternating lines of tetrameter (4 feet) and trimeter (3 feet). The ballad may have any number of stanzas in order to explore a story in some depth. The traditional ballad will also include an envoy in the form of a brief couplet or four-line stanza, which serves to bring the poem to a conclusion.

Modern forms of the ballad may use many types of meter and varying lengths of lines. The use of enjambment – the running of one stanza into the next - is quite acceptable and may help to keep the story flowing.

BALLAD OF LIFE

*Though there are many plans we make
to see us on our way,
and many promises we break
when we are led astray.*

*Though there are many silent dreams,
which haunt us in the night –
and many convoluted schemes,
which never seem quite right.*

*Though there is much to think about
and much that we might do.
Though we are touched by shades of doubt
to see the journey through.*

*The way before us is but brief
and prizes won are few –
and time becomes the final thief
that takes all that was true.*

*Then let us travel as we may
and keep our spirits bright.
Enjoy each moment of the day
nor fear the coming night.*

The Ballade

The ballade developed in France during the 14th century, and quickly appeared in England, in the work of writers such as Geoffrey Chaucer. Formal rules were introduced by Henri de Croi in 1493, when many forms of the ballade came into being. In keeping with its derivation from former songs of the same name, the written ballade was confined to three stanzas, usually of eight lines, and an envoy.

The aim of the ballade was to tell a story in the three main stanzas, whilst an envoy (often of fewer lines than the other stanzas) would finally address the subject of the story: a few words of praise for the hero, perhaps, or some moral implication to be drawn from what had been described. All stanzas, including the envoy, would be linked by a refrain line.

Lines might be of any length although iambic tetrameter or iambic pentameter was often the preferred choice. Of the many types of ballade, there are a few that have survived the years and this form of poetry is seen less often in modern poetry.

The (Standard) Ballade

Whilst the ballade may be written in many forms, best known of these is the (standard) ballade with three (eight-line) stanzas and final envoy. From previous notes, we know the ballade stanza has rhyme endings as shown:
>> **ababbcbc**

The (standard) ballade therefore, with final refrain lines for each stanza (including the envoy) then becomes:

>> **ababbcbC, ababbcbC, ababbcbC, bcbC**

It will be evident from the number of lines and choice of just three rhyme endings, that these soon become fairly obvious, and tend to fly in the face of modern rhyming poetry where the aim is to disguise any obvious or intrusive rhyme.

Both the length and use of repetitive rhyme, therefore, may well account for a decline of the (standard) ballade in contemporary poetry. However it does present the poet with a challenge and, used to good effect, may result in an interesting poem.

LOVE'S LAST FAREWELL

Beyond dark shadows, deep and green,
a forest pathway wanders through
where ancient beeches bend and lean,
to screen the cloudy sky from view.
Along a woodland avenue,
where hidden sorrow seems to dwell
of some forgotten rendezvous
where lovers met to say farewell.

Here, where a worn track runs between
a silent realm of morning dew:
untrodden ways, which once had seen
a place where gentle beauty grew.
A time when love was ever-true
long...long ago: a magic spell
that lingers, where warm breezes blew
and lovers met to say farewell.

This place that whispers what has been
and tainted with the residue
of broken dreams: this tragic scene
of promised hope, here torn in two.
Nor of time passing hitherto
that may, with lingering grace, dispel
the sadness of a last adieu
from lovers, met to say farewell.

Beyond dark shadows, deep and green,
a morning chill, which seems to tell
of sorrow dwelling unforeseen –
where lovers met to say farewell.

It may be seen in the previous example of a (standard) ballade that the rhyme scheme for the envoy was slightly changed. This was done deliberately, in order to make the first line of the envoy a refrain of the first line of the poem, thus:

AbabbcbC, ababbcbC, ababbcbC, AcaC

Once again we are reminded of the way in which we may "bend" the rules, if we feel this will enhance the poem.

Double Ballade

The double ballade adds two more stanzas, giving a total of 44 lines, although having done so, the need for an envoi becomes optional.

The double ballade is therefore a choice between

ababbcbC, ababbcbC, ababbcbC, ababbcbC, ababbcbC, bcbC

or
ababbcbC, ababbcbC, ababbcbC, ababbcbC, ababbcbC

Whatever choice we may make, it is evident that this will result in a fairly long poem. Since the general aim of poetry is to express a thought or an idea as succinctly as possible, then we might assume that the double ballade is unlikely to be considered unless we have some epic tale to tell.

Even if this holds true, we must then face the inevitable constraint of just three rhyme endings, as well as the need for a final refrain line for each stanza.

The Ballade Royal

As we would expect, the ballade royal is made from rhyme royal stanzas, with a slightly unique construction, whereby the envoy is of the same construction as the preceding stanzas. Thus:

ababbcC, ababbcC, ababbcC, ababbcC,

However, as for all forms of ballade, the first three stanzas are required to tell the story, whilst the envoy is provided to address the main subject of the poem, with a suitable summary. Another feature of the ballade royal is that the lines may be in either iambic tetrameter or iambic pentameter.

A SUMMER'S DAY

I should be working this fine Summer's day -
my desk beside the window duly spread
with papers piled in troubled disarray,
as if with patience waiting to be read
or filed again for reference ahead...
Yet just beyond my window, free of care,
bright butterflies float on the breathless air.

And there is much to do this Summer's day
before I find my weary way to bed.
Yet such sweet fragrance and the soft bouquet
of floral beauty from the flower bed...
and such fine notes from songsters overhead
that sing in praise of Summer's beauty fair.
Bright butterflies float on the breathless air.

Enough... enough! Let no more thoughts betray
my one declared intent, nor fill my head
with further musing this fine Summer's day.
So to my task - as if content instead
to spend my busy hours as I have said
absorbed in work, and therefore unaware
bright butterflies float on the breathless air.

Yet who is there who can deny a day
of such rare beauty? Let us then, instead,
enjoy an idle time as best we may.
For other days will come when joys have fled
and, bent to toil, we may then seek to thread
our thoughts back to this day... and future prayer:
bright butterflies float on the breathless air.

The Ballade Supreme

The ballade supreme has three ten-line stanzas to tell the story and a final envoy of five lines. Supreme indeed, having now grown to 36 lines, and clearly intended for the recounting of some great saga. The revised rhyme scheme is now as follows:

> **ababbccdcD, ababbccdcD, ababbccdcD, ccdcD**

or

> **ababbccdcD, ababbccdcD, ababbccdcD, ccdccD**

It will be seen that the ballade supreme now allows for four rhyme endings, although with the increased number of lines, this is hardly any easier to achieve. The need to find a dozen appropriate "c" rhymes, for example, may result in a restricted choice and lead to the desperate use of "inappropriate" rhymes.

This may be alleviated by introducing more refrain lines such as a repeated couplet to each stanza:

> **ababbccdCD, ababbccdCD, ababbccdCD, ccdCD**

The Double Ballade Supreme

We might hardly suppose that the ballade could grow any larger, until we finally arrive at the double ballade supreme, which adds another two stanzas, and (as before) the optional addition of an envoy. This has now reached epic proportions, and gives a poem of 55 lines, with only four possible rhyme endings, as follows:

> **ababbccdcD, ababbccdcD, ababbccdcD, ababbccdcD, ababbccdcD, ccdcD**

or

> **ababbccdcD, ababbccdcD, ababbccdcD, ababbccdcD, ababbccdcD**

It is hardly surprising to learn that the double ballade supreme is found mainly in former classical epic poems, and is rarely seen in modern poetry, although this should not necessarily deter anyone from "giving it a try" if so inclined.

Rondels, Rondeaus, Roundels, Rondelets and Roundelays

In the same tradition as ballads and ballades, which were originally sung by travelling minstrels, the rondeau and rondel also had their French origin in the tradition of songs and social gatherings. Their distinction from ballades and ballads lay in a more relaxed form, although they do include refrain lines. This, as we know, would originally have allowed the audience to join in with a rousing chorus, though we would hardly expect this now during a poetry recital!

Rondel

Originally a form of 14th century French poetry, the rondel has fourteen lines with just two rhyme endings, including two refrain lines which appear three times in total

ABba abAB abb aAB

or

ABab baAB aba bAB

Division of the poem into stanzas will traditionally follow the rhyme schemes as shown, but some flexibility is seen in modern versions.

Rondeau

The rondeau is of French origin and is usually a 15-line poem, divided into three stanzas. Refrain lines occur at the end of the 2nd and 3rd stanzas, and may be in the form of a phrase (or even just the first word) taken from the first line of the poem. This could well have been a chorus for everyone to join in at a time when rondeaus were sung. The poem is usually in iambic meter, although this may vary in modern versions.

(Ra)abba aabR aabbaR

where (Ra) is a single line, of which the first word or phrase (R) is repeated in later refrain lines .

Ten-Line Rondeau

The ten-line rondeau consists of two stanzas, each ending in a single word refrain taken from the first word of the poem. This actually gives twelve lines to the poem, although the single word refrains are not recognised as lines!

(Ra)bbaabR abbaR

where (Ra) is a single line, of which the first word (R) is repeated at the end of the both stanzas.

Rondeau Redouble

The rondeau redouble is an expanded variation of the rondeau, made longer to include five quatrains (four lines) and a final quintet (five lines). All four lines of the opening stanza provide refrain lines, which then appear in the stanzas that follow (as shown in the notation below). The concluding quintet also includes a final refrain line, which is intended as an echo of a phrase or complete line taken from the first line of the poem.

This is possibly not quite as complicated as it might sound.

$$A^1B^1A^2B^2 \; abaA^1 \; abaB^1 \; abaA^2 \; abaB^2 \; ababA^1$$

Roundel

Just to add to the confusion slightly, we also have the roundel. This is another variation of the rondeau, introduced by the Victorian poet Algernon Charles Swinburne (1837-1909). The poem has eleven lines, where a phrase from the first line is repeated as a refrain in the 4th and 11th lines. For example:

(Ra)baR bab abaR

where (Ra) is a single line, of which the first phrase (R) is repeated in later refrain lines.

It is possible to have the initial phrase (R) with the same rhyme ending as the second line (b) in which case the rhyme scheme becomes as shown:
(Ba)baB bab abaB

IF YOU LOVE ME

If you love me... love me true –
as true as any love might be,
likewise will be my love for you
if you love me.

And free of all uncertainty
to show my love, than hitherto
was ever seen in poetry.

Yet, at the start, when all is new
and I may doubt the signs I see,
I hesitate to seek a clue
if you love me.

The roundel works equally well as a single stanza poem, where the refrain line appears to occur quite naturally at various intervals

ODELESS

The day dawned bright – but not for me
with deeds to do and words to write,
yet lacking any clarity.
The day dawned bright:
as bright as any new day might,
though cloudy thoughts and lethargy
had filled my mind... a fading light
lost in some swirling alchemy.
And yet, despite my failed delight –
despite my listless energy,
the day dawned bright.

Rondelet

As the name implies, the rondelet is similar to the rondel but with only seven lines. The first line is repeated as a refrain in the third and final line, and should be shorter in length than other lines, although some latitude is allowed in modern versions.

AbAabbA

This shorter format is also well suited to modern rhyming poetry, as the following examples show.

LOVE LONG AGO

*Our children think that love is new
and something only they might know.
Our children think that love is new
because it seems so bright and true –
though we knew of it long ago.
Yet love is for the young, and so
our children think that love is new.*

The example above is in iambic meter, but the rondelet also works well if speeded up slightly as, for example, would be achieved using a dactylic meter in the following poem. This also serves to show again how the mood of a poem is influenced by the meter.

WINE

*Never drink wine in the heat of the day.
Seek out the shade of a cool forest glade,
but never drink wine in the heat of the day.
For dreaming will follow and lead you astray
through a hushed, drowsy calm of ambition betrayed,
where thoughts of your afternoon work will soon fade.
No... never drink wine in the heat of the day.*

Roundelay

To complete the picture, we have the roundelay, which originated as a very loosely controlled song with a chorus. This has now come to be a short, simple rhyming poem with no formal structure at all, other than some frequent repetition of a refrain line.

ICE AND FIRE

Ice and fire: the sparkling white
of candles and remembrance bright
whose silent tongues of golden flames
tell now of unforgotten names
and those at rest this Christmas Eve.

Ice and fire – a sea of light
like stars that flicker through the night
above the cemetery, where
all loved ones, past and present, share
a time of joy at Christmas Eve.

The celebrated golden glow
of candles burning in the snow,
except where older pathways stray:
where none return to pause or pray –
no candles lit at Christmas Eve.

Dark corners with no bright flame blessed
of twice forgotten souls at rest:
the dead forgotten by the dead
while silent pools of darkness spread
with none to come and none to grieve
for some at rest this Christmas Eve.

ARRIVAL ROUNDELAY

They came...the first: they came with gold
part hidden by the morning mist,
which drifted slowly, damp and cold.
Yet with a wonder softly kissed
they came...their beauty to behold.

And others followed, dressed in white,
like snowflakes on a cloth of green
and gleaming in the morning light.
From hidden places never seen
they came... the first: of white and gold.

And more...the final few we saw
in regal colours finely shown
awoken, that we gazed in awe
where graceful crocuses had grown.
They came...the purple, white and gold.

Triolet, Villanelle and Pantoum

Triolet

Many other remaining traditional forms of poetry are derived from former song performances and it is with little surprise, therefore, that they too include the frequent use of refrain lines and limited rhyme endings.

The triolet, is of French origin, and the first known example is that of "The Cléomadès" by Adenès Le Roi (1258 - 1297). The name is something of a misnomer, since it might well suggest a combination of three-line stanzas, although the triple aspect of this poem is in reference to the triple repetition of a refrain line. The poem is quite brief with only one stanza of eight lines, and is limited to just two rhyme endings including several refrain lines:

ABaAabAB

We may think of this construction as **(ABa + A + abA + B)** which perhaps hints at its original derivation, although to do so makes it no easier to write.

The use of so many refrain lines in such a small number of lines is difficult, but if this was not already enough of a challenge, the triolet is also intended to provide an opportunity for a play on words. This may be achieved from lines which imply a subtle change of emphasis, or would even include words of a similar sound, but having different meanings. This might also allow the use of puns or other amusing devices, although it must be said that the triolet will often become as much a technical challenge as a work of poetical inspiration.

It is not surprising to discover that the triolet is rarely seen as a popular form of modern poetry. In the example that follows, the rhyme scheme has been changed slightly:

ABbAbbAB   (ABb + A + bbA + B)

so that technically it is not really a triolet at all!

However, we return to the bending of rules and the fact that this modified rhyme scheme is seen to work quite well, so no-matter what we may call it, this is still a poem of eight lines with a triple refrain.

FORTY YEARS AGO

*When (forty years ago) we thought
we said goodbye...it was not so.
Though at the time we did not know
how, forty years ago, we thought
we might find romance to bestow
a time to stay: how love would grow
from forty years ago. We thought
we said goodbye - it was not so.*

Villanelle

The villanelle was originally a "round song" sung by French medieval farm labourers, (from the Latin "villa" meaning farm). As such, the original form lacked any real structure, other than a simple rhyme scheme and the inclusion of frequent refrain lines, allowing the audience to join in with the chorus.

However, this irregular construction was to evolve later into a more disciplined form during the 16th century.

The villanelle is written in tercets (3 line stanzas) and will usually have five in total, although more pairs of stanzas may be added to create an epic poem. In all cases, however, the final stanza takes the form of a quatrain, with a double refrain

The villanelle has the following rhyme scheme:

$$A^1 b A^2 \quad ab A^1 \quad ab A^2 \quad ab A^1 \quad ab A^2 \quad ab A^1 A^2$$

where **A^1** and **A^2** are separate (rhyming) refrain lines.

VILLANELLE RHYME

I like the villanelle, and this is true –
for mostly with refrain lines here and there
one only has to write a line or two.

This seems to be an easy thing to do,
in terms of other lines one must prepare.
I like the villanelle, and this is true.

So barely started then – yet halfway through
requiring little thought and little care.
One only has to write a line or two.

The rhymes fall into place, as if on cue.
What fun indeed – I really do declare
I like the villanelle, and this is true.

Though as I carry on the words grow few,
and I must struggle then, although aware
one only has to write a line or two.

Then with relief the end comes into view
and happy with the words I write and share.
I like the villanelle, and this is true....
one only has to write a line or two!

There are only two rhymes used throughout the poem, which may explain the usual limit of six stanzas in total. Once again the refrain lines form an essential feature of the poem, and repeated at intervals this does allow a little "breathing space" to lessen their impact, although they remain clearly discernible throughout.

Some surprising good effects are possible from this construction, particularly in the way that the final refrain couplet tends to "round-off" the poem and echo back to the start , as shown above.

The Pantoum

The pantoum is a long way from home, and comes originally from Malaya. It was introduced into Europe in 1820 by the German poet Adelbert von Chamisso (1781 - 1838), and became popular for a short while.

The rhyme scheme is as follows, and shows one redeeming feature in the way that the poem is seen to complete a loop, returning to where it started:

$$A^1B^1\ A^2B^2\ B^1C^1\ B^2C^2\ C^1D^1\ C^2D^2\ D^1E^1\ D^2E^2\ E^1A^2\ E^2A^1$$

PANTOUM OF TIME

Time has new meaning now – days come and go
with lesser urgency than once we knew.
This rhythm, which our lives have come to know
of less ambition, and of things to do
with lesser urgency than once we knew.
It is enough, to fill each passing day
of less ambition, and of things to do
from interesting tasks that come our way.
It is enough to fill each passing day
like echoes of a soft, repeated rhyme
from interesting tasks that come our way,
with casual observation at the time.
Like echoes of a soft, repeated rhyme
and idle moments, knowing it must be
with casual observation at the time.
This gentle pace, with time to pause and see
and idle moments, knowing it must be
this rhythm which our lives have come to know.
This gentle pace, with time to pause and see
time has new meaning now – days come and go.

Unfortunately the pantoum finds little favour in modern poetry, primarily due to the frequency of refrain lines which tend to produce a rather stilted effect. Since every line in the poem becomes a refrain line, this is something akin to someone having said something and then repeating themselves. Slight variations in the refrain lines can help, although this still remains something of a restriction.

With the usual aim in poetry of being to achieve a smooth flow of words, this becomes exceeding difficult in the pantoum without appearing slightly contrived. There are, however, no rules with regard to meter or length of lines, allowing some slight variation.

PANTOUM OF LOVE

I am in love with you – you know it so.
The love I have declared in gentle rhyme
repeated and repeated – for we know
how love fills every moment of our time.
The love I have declared in gentle rhyme
is but the smallest part of all I feel:
how love fills every moment of our time.
This poem then, which true love may reveal,
is but the smallest part of all I feel.
This truth of constant love, yet there may come
a poem then, which true love may reveal –
though cannot, even so, attempt to plumb
this truth of constant love. Yet there may come
such words as may an honesty convey –
though cannot, even so, attempt to plumb
the depth of all I feel. I need not say
such words as may an honesty convey
repeated and repeated – for we know
the depth of all I feel. I need not say
I am in love with you...you know it so.

The Curtal Sonnet, Kyrielle and Lai

The Curtal Sonnet

The curtal sonnet is a poem of eleven lines (which is quite odd in itself) and was devised by Gerard Manley Hopkins (1844 - 1889). Since we invariably think of a sonnet as having fourteen lines, we need to remind ourselves that the word "sonnet" derives from the Italian meaning a "little song". The word "curt" is also defined as being discourteously brief, which may provide another hint to the name.

There appears to be no "pattern" to the curious rhyme scheme:

abcabcdbcdc

Gerard Manley Hopkins is noted mainly for his original form of "sprung verse" (see earlier notes) and his preference for a traditional sonnet of fourteen lines with a rhyme scheme (**abba abba cdcdcd**). However, an excellent example of the curtal sonnet may be seen in his famous poem **"Pied Beauty"**

DAWN DARKNESS

The day grew darker with the coming dawn.
The full moon, westward, slowly passing by
had brightly shone throughout the glinting night
of crystal stars – their beauty then withdrawn
as early morning tinged the eastern sky.
Yet risen also came the pallid light
of grey mist, creeping over hedge and field:
a gathering of low cloud drifting by,
to shroud the dull horizon from our sight.
Dark then and darker was the dawn revealed,
than of the former moon's bright-silver flight.

Counting syllables

It is unusual in English or European poetry to concern ourselves with the counting of syllables. Quite often the use of a regular meter will, in itself, tend to regulate the number of syllables to be found in a line of poetry, but we don't normally count them. One possible modern exception will be when writing blank verse, where lines of equal (metric) length are used. As we have already seen, this tends to distinguish blank verse from free verse.

The strict counting of syllables (syllabic verse) is more often associated with forms of poetry arising from Japan and China, which we later consider. It is, however, not new to European poetry, and can be traced back to early medieval times.

Kyrielle

The kyrielle is a form of French medieval poetry. Traditionally the poem is written in couplets, arranged in quatrains (four lines), where each line has a count of eight syllables, usually in iambic tetrameter (4 feet). The main requirement is a refrain line for the fourth line of each stanza:
> **aabB ccbB ddbB** ...and so on

KYRIELLE OF SPRING

*The hazel catkins tremble where
the blue tits come to feed and play,
and spring is drifting in the air
this misty, grey awoken day.*

*Bright blue tits flutter through the air
with great excitement, to convey
a joy of which they are aware
this misty, grey awoken day.*

*And all around there seems to be
a time made wonderful and gay,
beyond what we might pause to see
this misty, grey awoken day.*

For shorter poems, the division between stanzas may be omitted to give a single stanza poems and a more continuous flow of words. Some variation in the quatrains of the kyrielle is allowed, which may include:

abaB cbcB dbdB ...and so on

MOMENTS LOST

*I write this for the memory
of dreams that we will never share.
The moments lost, that cannot be:
the times when I was never there.*

*The wasted days: the special few
when I was gone, and unaware
of all I might have shared with you -
the times when I was never there.*

*Alas... the lonely lane ahead
and lonely thoughts, now filled with care -
when I shall now recall instead
the times when I was never there.*

Lai

The lai is another form of medieval French poetry of an obscure origin, but revived during the 17th century. It has nine lines and a deceptively simple rhyme scheme

aabaabaab

However, once again we need to count syllables, where we find that all of the "a" rhymes are for lines of five syllables, whereas the "b" rhymes have lines of just two syllables. This can be quite dramatic and leads to a few sharp pauses along the way!

LAI

*I thought I might write
a poem quite bright
today.
It started alright
with thoughts that it might
convey.
The end soon in sight -
to my great delight
a Lai!*

Ode, Epic Poem, Elegy and Sestina

Having a somewhat dated connotation, any reference to an ode is taken to imply some slightly derisory comment on poetry. However, the ode deserves a little more respect, from its ancient Greek origin. An ode is the Greek word for "song" and is meant to imply an exalted style of poetry. There are two main types of the ode, as follows:

The Pindaric Ode

The Pindaric ode has a triadic (three-stanza) structure. The opening lines of the first stanza (strophe) were originally sung to set the theme of the poem, followed by the second stanza (antistrophe), which developed the story further. Finally the third stanza (epode) drew the poem to a conclusion. We might tend to think of this as a poem having a beginning, a middle, and an end!

Each stanza may be of any number of lines or rhyme scheme and tends to be quite simple. In developing a lengthy story, however, each of the three stanzas may require a great many lines. When odes were sung in ancient Greece, the performers danced to the left during the "strophe", then to the right during the antistrophe", and finally stood still during the "epode"

The Horatian Ode

The Horatian ode is usually "homostrophic", which is to say that it includes the introduction of a stanza, usually quite brief, which is repeated and presented in a particular way at intervals throughout the poem. This is often used to provide an on-going theme, especially in long or complicated odes.

Curiously, the ode was much favoured by English Romantic poets such as John Keats (1795 - 1821) "Ode to a Nightingale"; Percy Bysshe Shelley (1792 - 1822) "Ode to a Skylark" and William Wordsworth (1770 - 1850) "Ode: Imitations of Immortality"... all of whom had been educated with an appreciation of the Greek Classics.

The Modern Ode

The modern ode bears little resemblance to the more illustrious classical origins. It does, however, tell a story, which will often include some concluding observation. The modern ode also brings the anticipation of something amusing.

A QUIET NEET IN

It didn't start reet well as 'ow they 'adn't booked a'ead.
Th'otel 'ad no vacancies - they couldn't find a bed.
But Joe, 'e found a stable. Mary said as 'ow t'would do,
so while she took a nap Joe lit a fire an' 'ad a brew.

'E began t' feel more cheerful - Bethlehem wur quite a town,
but while Joe wur bearin' up 'e noticed Mary bearin' down.
The baby came wi'out much fuss - 'e 'ardly cried at all,
an' Mary seemed quite comf'table
when someone came t'call.

It wur three foreign travellers as 'ad journeyed from afar -
a curious navigation wot involved a movin' star.
Joe wurn't right certain wot t'do,
they men looked strange an' old,
but thought as 'ow they should come in when one said
"I bring gold."

An' 'appen t'other two seemed odd.
Joe wondered who they wur
an' wot t'do wi' gifts they brought o' frankincense an' myrrh?
They 'ung around fer quite a while an' Mary seemed alreet.
Yon baby slept an' Joe thought it 'ad been a funny neet.

An' then, just when it seemed as 'ow t'wur time
t'get some sleep,
some shepherds wandered in
wi' a small flock o' smelly sheep.
They said they'd been up in't yon 'ills an' saw a shinin' leet,
an' 'eard a voice proclaimin' like it wur a special neet...
an' Joe began t' think as 'ow they shepherds wur nay breet.

*'E let 'em stay awhile - it wur reet clear they wur impressed
wi' baby an' wi' wise ol' men as wur so smartly dressed.
They chatted fer a while 'til Joe got fed up wi' a sheep
an' said "'Tis time you left, lads.
Me an' Mary needs us sleep."*

*Maybe if 'e 'ad known 'ow things wur later t' turn out,
e might 'ave 'ad a party... spent some gold on crates o' stout.
But 'appen 'twur a quiet neet in - or so it would appear.
An' who'd 'ave thought yon story
would survive two thousan' year!*

Epic Poetry

An epic poem is written on a grand scale and is usually a lengthy narrative dealing with a natural topic, and/or the response of man in relation to nature. A good example of this would be "Paradise Lost" by John Milton (1608 - 1674).

Much like the ode, epic poetry is seldom to be found in modern times – it would seem that most folk prefer a good novel!

Elegy

An elegy is a poem written to lament or to honour a deceased person. In as much as great men and women come and go, there will always be solemn examples found of the elegy.

Ideally, an elegy should concern itself with a celebration and remembrance of the person, rather than dwelling too profoundly on their death.

EUCALYPTUS MEMORY
(In memory of Mike Bush)

The eucalyptus cuttings we were given still survive –
though little more than sticks with leaves and hopefully, alive.
A chilly breeze blows where they now grow planted in a row
and having, so it seems, survived the drifts of winter snow.

Three fragile sticks that bend like wire to every wayward gust;
three doubtful hopes that represent our tenancy of trust.
Yet of their slender nature stirs the thought of what may be,
that from this tender gift there will be one grows to a tree.

The winter-tide has come and gone –
and come and gone our friend
who spoke of spring and daffodils,
and days that we might spend
together in the sunshine...yes, when he would come to see
the view where later there would grow a eucalyptus tree.

He did not know how cancer then had rooted at his core –
how he might count the winter days
and know of nothing more.
The visit I had made...an idle conversation shared
that spoke of more than what was said
with quiet smiles prepared.

There is a corner of our field where thin sticks slowly grow –
a place we visit now and then,
with thoughts that come and go
of someone we remember and of how things come to be:
that one day we may stand beneath a eucalyptus tree.

The Sestina

The sestina is a form of poetry invented by the French poet Arnaut Daniel (1180 - 1200) in the late 12th century. It has a complicated structure and achieved little recognition, although a brief renewed interest was shown in France and England during the 19th century.

The name is derived from the fact that the sestina has six stanzas, each of six lines (sestet), followed by a stanza of three lines (tercet). There is no rhyme within the stanzas, and the sestina depends instead on a structured recurrent pattern for the repetition of word endings.

In its original form, each line was of ten syllables, although the sestina has since undergone many changes throughout its development. Acceptable modern forms show lines of varying lengths.

The recurrent end-word pattern is such that each successive stanza is based on reverse pairing of lines from the preceding stanza, taking the (1st & 6th),(2nd & 5th), (3rd & 4th). If this is starting to sound complicated (and it is) then it may be easier to simply follow the pattern below:

```
1 2 3 4 5 6
6 1 5 2 4 3
3 6 4 1 2 5
5 3 2 6 1 4
4 5 1 3 6 2
2 4 6 5 3 1
```

The final tercet must include all of the six line endings as mid-line and end-line positions. The pattern for this tercet is as shown below, although the mid-line position (shown in brackets) need not, necessarily, be exactly midway.

(2)5 (4)3 (6)1

Clearly this rigid structure, as well as the aim of ten syllables to each line, can be something of a mathematical and intellectual challenge, although despite such efforts it often struggles in the true aim of poetry, which is surely to write in a way that appeals to various aesthetic and emotional qualities.

However, if this appeals to you, then why not give it a try?

Greek Poetry

We have already acknowledged that the ancient Greeks did much to define various types of poetry, both in terms of types of meter (many of which are not readily suited to the English language) and also in terms of the frequently complicated combinations of various meters into recognised forms.

A summary of Greek meters is provided on page 265.

So numerous are such examples, that we might readily devote an entire chapter to this topic alone. However, for the most part, these meters are rarely encountered or even appreciated in English poetry.

This is not to say that they have not been attempted, with great competency, from time to time by some of our famous poets. John Milton (1608 - 1674) and Alfred Lord Tennyson (1809 - 1892), for example, are both known to have written lengthy poems in the Greek style of alcaics, a complicated mix of iambs, trochees and dactyls.

The sapphic is also a classical Greek four-line stanza of non-rhyming lines attributed to the poetess Sappho, which we have already considered in the earlier section on stanza forms (see page 120).

Whilst not wishing to simply dismiss or assign some of these Greek forms of poetry construction as lost in the distant past, it is still true to observe that they are scarcely ever seen in modern English poetry. For that reason alone, we will not pursue them further, although we should acknowledge them to be the origin of all modern poetry.

Our construction and understanding of many of the subtle aspects of a poem are attributed to the scholarship of these early poets, and form the platform upon which poetry has developed throughout each period of history. It is sufficient, perhaps, to know of their existence, should we ever be tempted to wander in this direction at some future time.

Welsh Poetry

The Welsh are renowned for their skill and love of poetry, dating back to their Celtic origins. Poetry written chiefly in the Welsh language restricts any broad appreciation of their culture, although as with other sources of inspiration from various places and periods in history, it is always possible to adopt some salient feature of construction, and try it for ourselves.

Welsh poetry is composed within very strict guidelines, which are frequently associated with rules concerning the number of syllables and an essential introduction of cross-rhyming.

Awdl Gywydd

The Awdl Gywydd (owdl gôw-widd) is a typical example with quatrain stanzas and a count of seven syllables to each line.

The ending for line 1 will find a matching internal rhyme with (3rd, 4th or 5th) syllables of line 2.

Similarly, the ending for line 3 will find a matching internal rhyme with (3rd, 4th or 5th) syllables of line 4.

Finally, to draw the stanza together, the ending of lines 2 and 4 must also rhyme.

As we can see, this starts to become quite complicated, but may be shown as follows...

a(ab)c(cb)

where (ab) is a single line, of which the first part (a) is an internal rhyme
and likewise (cb) is a single line, of which the first part (c) is an internal rhyme.

RED DRAGONS

In this green and ancient land:
in this land of magic spells –
hidden caves, where close at hand
all dark arts and secrets dwell.

Fables few men understand
of red dragons and a time
of old Merlin - tales once heard:
written words in books of rhyme.

Ancient runes and Celtic lore
known before, which since have lain
till old days return once more,
and red dragons roar again.

The poem that follows is an attempted allusion to the use of words reminiscent of Dylan Thomas (1914 - 1953) in his famous poem "Fern Hill", although the unique style of this poet is exceedingly difficult to emulate.

HAPPY IN MY TIME

Happy in my time I grew
beneath skies blue in heydays
of a summer, ever bright
in delightful childhood ways.

Young of limb - an innocence
in the confidence of youth,
and the dawning day made long
in the gentle song of truth.

Lovely then among the fields
and the yielding hour squandered
where tall foxgloves came again,
along the lane I wandered.

Happy and free as a lark
in the spark of first knowing
how the days may sometimes pass
fair as the green grass growing.

And the whispering of trees
and the green seas... cliff and sand,
where I ran and sang and strayed
through dreams made in that fair land.

Heedless then as a young child
in wonder wild and delight,
I grew through my golden age
in an ageless realm of light.

Lovely then and now... the days
lost in a haze of distance
and memories come again:
though they come again by chance.

MODERN POETRY

Acrostic, Telestich, Alphabetical

It would be wrong to suggest that many of the so-called "traditional poems" we have considered cannot still be regarded as modern poems. Clearly they owe their origin to ancient roots, but they are alive and well, and continue to bring us bright flowers of wonder and imagination.

However, poetry is a living thing, and in much the same way as all forms of art evolve and develop, so too poetry has seen many changes. Many of these arise from an up-dating of more traditional forms, particularly with the relaxation of former rules. Why, for example, should all sonnets be written in iambic pentameter, when we know that a different meter may provide a complete change of mood in the poem?

We may also be influenced by the poetry from other countries in forms that we may never have considered. This has happened in the past with poems now considered quite English (such as the sonnet, for example) and seems likely to continue. We will later consider recent developments arising from a greater awareness of poetry originating from the Far East.

Other new forms of expression are continually evolving as a result of experimentation, along with an occasional dash of inspiration. It is the fun aspect of poetry, which we have accepted from the very start of this book as an integral part of what we set out to achieve.

Use of Metaphor

The use of metaphor plays an important part of modern poetry, through the juxtapositioning and representation of attributes and character. The poem **"Love Story"** that follows shows one such example of the way that this may be achieved.

LOVE STORY

*He was a summer breeze –
she was a gentle sigh
whispering softly between the tall trees.
He was the warming sun –
she was the moonlight won,
charmed with the magic of a loving ease.*

*He was the turning tide...
she was the distant sky
shimmering brightly, so blue and so wide.
He was a steady rhyme
spoken of passing time.
She was the passion he felt inside.*

*He was the guiding theme –
she was the reason why.
He was the architect of their dream
built on a mutual plan.
She was the talisman
bringing good fortune to life's steady stream.*

*He was the wandering way
taken as time passed by.
She was the dawning of another day.
He was the constant shield...
never to bend or to yield.
She was the promise he could not betray.*

*She was the autumn gold.
He was the sudden goodbye –
dark as the night of a long winter's cold.
He was the memory
of summer's lost harmony.
She was a love story still to be told.*

*He was the page of stone
telling how love cannot die.
She was an afternoon wandering alone,
there...in that quiet place.
He was the feeling of grace,
lingering now with the time they had known.*

Playing with Words

There are many other ways in which we can use language: ways that may serve to introduce some subtle aspect to the poem, as well as occasionally fulfilling a sense of technical achievement.

We will consider a few of the more popular types of poetry, some of which include a hidden message or meaning in their clever construction.

Acrostic Poem

The acrostic poem is one where a word or phrase is spelt out (reading downwards) by the first letter of each line. This should be quite subtle, and may well pass un-noticed until attention is drawn to the fact, as shown in the poem **"Valentine Rhyme"** (page 82).

Telestich Poem

The telestich poem is similar to the acrostic, except that a word or phrase is spelt out by the last letter of each line. For rhyming poetry, attempting to achieve the same phonetical sounds from words with different endings can be even more of a challenge. The telestich may also not be recognised, as shown in the example that follows:

> ***JUBILATION***
>
> *I have been stirred upon a fresh debut,*
> *although uncertain yet of what to do –*
> *and so I wait, prepared with ink and nib*
> *to scribble freely with glib energy.*
>
> *Yet with a jubilation, bright and new,*
> *to view what few have seen – the fine and fair*
> *ambition, of which I am made aware,*
> *whilst inching forward slowly I begin.*

Double Acrostic Poem

The double acrostic poem simply combines the challenges of acrostic and telestich to spell out the same word or phrase. This is, in fact, far from simple to achieve, but well worth the effort.

GHOSTS

*Ghosts are waking - phantoms floatin*g,
*haunting ruins... drifting throug*h.
*Omens dark with warnings to*o!
*Spectral souls and apparition*s -
*troubled wraiths of grim debu*t
*stirred to each grave rendezvou*s.

Note: A deliberate pun is included in the above poem with its reference to a "grave" rendezvous.

Compound Acrostic

A compound acrostic poem is similar to the double acrostic, with hidden vertical words or phrases included in the first and last letters of each line, but differs in as much as the chosen message (read from top to bottom) will be different for each side.

To work properly there must also be some relationship between the two vertical lines, as shown in the following example.

TAROT

(the prediction of life's fortune and direction)

Not everyone, in manner apropos,
observes from destiny the way to go –
reaching in life some bleak and lost plateau.
Too late...their fate not foreseen in tarot,
hope finds them lost: as was true of Van Gogh.

Each journey is a mystery, we know,
and we may come upon both friend or foe –
so always then, in manner apropos,
to seek direction not found in tarot.

Alphabetical Verse

I am certain that other poets will have written poems of twenty-six lines, where each line begins with the next letter in the alphabet, although I have yet to come across this in print. Perhaps it is something peculiar to my own ambitions.

The challenges, of course, will be encountered by lines that begin with awkward letters, such as "q" or "x", although the tendency then is to apply a phonetical approach. Other letters may also be awkward, particularly since they need to be faced at each appropriate line as the poem progresses.

The added difficulty is in achieving a flow of words, particularly when the need for rhyme and a degree of disguise at the start of the lines is required... none of which is easy. Added to which, all such technical merit may well pass unseen as happened in the following example, which was entered into a competition.

One other aspect of alphabetic verse is the fact that it provides a series of convenient four-line stanzas, together with a concluding couplet.

AUTUMN CONFETTI

Autumn confetti – the yellow leaves falling,
brittle as parchment: the saga of trees.
Coppery flakes of past summer recalling –
downward they tumble and swirl in the breeze.

Eddies of air lift each amber ambition:
fragments of history scattered around.
Gilded by sunlight, this brief exhibition:
hovering...tumbling to carpet the ground.

In the dark forest of skeletal branches,
jagged black silhouettes stabbing the sky.
Keenly the rime of a white hoar frost blanches
leaves that await their brief moment to fly.

Memories fade with a poignant aroma.
Nonchalance drifts into depths of decay.
Overt acceptance of chill winter's coma:
pliant defeat of a vanquished display.

Quietly now comes the hush of expectance.
Russet leaves rest beneath whispering trees.
Secrets rehearsed with repeated acceptance.
Tales carried forth on the autumnal breeze.

Unwritten legends, like golden rings hidden.
Viscous sap draining to roots dark below.
Waiting the winter, of verdure forbidden,
exiled to slumber as seasons bestow.

Yellow confetti: the autumn leaves falling.
Zodiac omens...the cycles recalling.

Mixed Meter, Logaoedic and Macaronic Verse

We know from our study of various meters, that these may be freely mixed under certain circumstances, to add pace and drama to what is being said. We have also seen how some traditional forms of poetry require the strict use of certain types of meter and certain lengths of line. For example, the sonnet should have fourteen lines in iambic pentameter.

The indiscriminate mixing of meter is more likely to occur in free verse, although here too some consideration of normal speech must prevail, if the lines are to scan properly. Amongst the best-known examples of deliberate (possibly awkward) mixed meter will be the "sprung verse" of Gerard Manley Hopkins (1844 - 1889), which we have already considered under the use of meter (see page 52). An example of sprung verse is shown in a sonnet "**Everlong**" (page 157).

Logaoedic Poem

The logaoedic poem also features mixed meter and may be composed of all forms. The success of such a mêlée will depend entirely on a need for the words to flow in a controlled manner.

>   **WHAT WORDS ARE THESE**
>
>   *What words are these...wrought of an ancient art?*
>   *This penmanship and a hesitant start.*
>
>   *What words...what words of dull repetition seen?*
>   *What inversion between rhymes irregular*
>   *and meter flawed:*
>   *existing...yet mostly ignored*
>
>   *What words indeed, of a critical view?*
>   *Enjambment of stanzas, with a modern and new*
>
>   *sophistication – here, in the true sense.*
>   *What words of confusion and shallow pretence?*

Macaronic Verse

We live in a world where movement between countries and cultures has become a common thing, exposing us to all manner of foreign languages and, hopefully, a gradual understanding of them. This has been reflected in poetry, from time to time, both in terms of translations and the use of other languages.

Macaronic verse may also be used in a burlesque form for amusement, and may include Latin as well as other foreign or vernacular words.

The problem with a mix of languages is that attempts at translation from one to the other may often result in a loss of meaning or understanding of the poetical aspects. We may understand the words, but poetry evolves from the way in which words are put together, both in terms of how they reflect one another and often in the manner by which they chime together.

VOILÀ TOUT

It seems, my love, that we grow old
although our love remains as true,
yet gentler now, perhaps less bold
than was the love that we once knew –
surtout des anciens rendezvous.
Though embers glow with burning gold
to bring the warmth I share with you,
and kisses then, a thousand-fold
of love that we may yet pursue –
il y a entre nous et jusqu'au bout.

Then let it be that we grow old
along an autumn avenue,
that of our days we then behold
how love remains as bright and new –
tout ce que je veux avec toi.

Notes on the previous poem:

> *surtout des anciens rendezvous. (from our past meetings)*
> *il y a entre nous et jusqu'au bout. (between us until the end)*
> *tout ce que je veux avec toi. (and that is all I wish with you)*

Macaronic verse is a form of poetry which combines lines or phrases written in different languages. The success that this might achieve is restricted to the degree by which it may be readily understood. One will hardly want to have a language translation dictionary available to read the poem, and the aim may be to provide a meaning in terms of the context of the word.

Alternatively, the poet might seek to provide a suggested translation from the combined repetition of words or phrases in both languages, or in the form of footnotes.

Often the inclusion of a foreign language will be confined to a word or short phrase, and may be intended simply as an amusing bilingual pun or words of some jumbled meaning. However, a more serious aspect from combined languages may be to add atmosphere.

C'EST COMME C'EST

> *It is as it is – et c'est comme c'est.*
> *It is as we hoped it would be.*
> *From the dawning of another day*
> *and all that we hoped to see.*
> *De l'aube au crepuscule pour nous:*
> *from dawn to dusk for me and you.*
>
> *Like this...like that; comme çi, comme ça*
> *the seasons slowly pass us by*
> *with idle charm – je ne sais quoi*
> *how quickly then the hours fly.*
> *Yet this is all we hoped would be*
> *from dawn to dusk, for you and me.*

Comedy

Comedy in verse

It is often tempting to emulate the style of some well-known poet, if only to learn from this. Pretentious works are always a temptation, when it comes to a more satirical approach. We have already looked at this form of allusion in poetry, but it may serve well to remind ourselves of a few subtle differences.

Parody

In attempting to emulate another style, the poet may well come to gain a great appreciation of the skills and techniques necessary to achieve this, which can be no bad thing. Sometimes, however, a subsequent imitation may be of a more critical nature, with a "sting in the tail".

Where this occurs, the poem becomes a parody – something that mimics another poet's poem or style in a more satirical manner. If intended as a light-hearted piece of verse, this may well be regarded as a harmless spoof, although there are many shades of parody, which may also target the original poet in some more personal way.

Pastiche

The pastiche is a literary work composed of material or of a distinctive form that allows it to be identified with other known sources. This is quite important, in order to avoid any suggestion of plagiarism or the implication that some particularly inspired poem, albeit in a modified form, is that of our own creation.

In earlier notes we have seen how allusion may be used to show respect to some former original poem, and may seek to develop further a particular theme or idea. The pastiche may be written in the same style or use the same language as some greater known work, but should still find something new to say. Where possible its aim will often be to draw humour from any such comparison with the original poem by means of a play on words, in what might be a more relaxed or even flippant style.

NOAH AN' 'IS ARK

'E said 'is name wur Noah an' 'e'd cum t'buy some wood,
but when 'e placed 'is order - well, it wurn't reet understood.
So gaffer 'e wur summoned like t'lend an 'elping 'and
in the 'ope as 'ow as gaffer 'e at least would understand.

It seemed this chap called Noah 'ad a plan t'build a boat.
'E said it wur an ark...but it wur summat as would float.
An' in this ark 'e said 'e planned t' 'ave a ruddy zoo!
Well, gaffer 'e jus' nodded like as 'ow it wur 'e knew -
but thinkin' (quiet like) it wur a funny thing t'do.

Now Noah 'ad some plans as 'ow 'e let t'gaffer see;
about yon ark - dimensions like, wot showed 'ow it should be.
It wur fifty cubits wide an' it wur thirty cubits high
an' three 'undred cubits long...though Noah couldn't say jus' why.

Well gaffer 'e wur jiggered, an' I saw 'im scratch 'is 'ead.
"We ain't got nowt in't cubits - we've gone metric now," 'e said.
So they 'ad t'work it out as jus' 'ow long a cubit wur,
an' it come t'twenty inches... gi' or tak' some 'ere and thur.

"We'd best call it 'arf a metre, this 'ere cubit," gaffer said.
An' Noah said, "Aye... appen that'll do reet fine instead."
So gaffer took 'is pencil wot 'e keeps behind 'is ear
an' scribbled on t'plans 'is metric sums t'mak' it clear.

By 'eck it took a while t'work out all they planks o' wood,
but gaffer persevered, as 'ow t'order wur reet good:
'til 'e asked t'chap called Noah jus' wot type o' wood would do -
but when Noah 'e said gopher wood it caused a reet t'do.

"Go fer wood," says gaffer, "But thar's come fer wood t'me."
"Nay... gopher wood," says Noah. "Wot grows on t'gopher tree."
Well, gaffer 'e wur jiggered once again, but gi' 'im due -
'e gave a smile, determined like, t'see wot 'e could do.

"We don't 'ave call fur gopher wood," 'e started t'explain.
"We've teak an' oak an' walnut - wot as got a lovely grain
but 'appens costs a lot o' brass...an' if this ark wur mine
I reckon I'd be 'appy like t'see it built in pine."
An' Noah 'e jus nodded an' said "'Appen pine is fine."

So gaffer took 'is pencil from behind 'is ear once more,
an' worked out what the cost wur as delivered door t'door.
An' seein' 'ow it come t'quite a sum (an' bein' nice)
'e let Noah 'ave it trade wi' a discount on t'price.

Well Noah thanked t'gaffer an' then said "If I wur thee
I'd build mysen an ark afore it starts t'rain thar see."
An' gaffer smiled an' said as 'ow 'e lived up on't yon 'ill
an' reckoned 'e'd not need a boat. An' Noah says, "Thar will."

+++++

Well that wur as it 'appened like, an' thar's 'eard I s'pose
as 'ow yon chap called Noah got 'is ark builded thar knows.
But when it come t'creatures like thur wur a reet t'do -
wi' neighbours none too 'appy like about 'is ruddy zoo.

'E 'ad whippets an' a ferret an' 'is pigeons an' a cat -
an' no-one really minded like not if'n that wur that.
'E 'ad 'ampsters an' a guinea pig an' a rabbit e' called Fluff -
an' even Missus Noah said she thought 'e 'ad enough...

but then 'e wen' an' bought an 'orse. It wur reet daft, but true.
So t'council man was summoned like t'see wot 'e could do.
"Thar can't keep 'orse in't garden, 'appen thar mus' understand
t'neighbours don't like noises an' t'smell is none too grand.

Well Noah wur reet sorry, an' t'council man said "Reet -
but t'other thing is ark, thar knows, 'tis blockin' 'arf t'street.
Thar dursn't leave it thur as 'ow 'tis not wur boat should be -
so's thar bes' mak' arrangements like t'tak' it down t'sea."

Well Noah wurn't reet 'appy an' 'e tried like t'explain,
but t'council man wur adamant an said "I'll mak' it plain -
thar needs t'get ark shifted an' I'll nay tell thee again..."
An' 'appen Noah will soon as we gets a break from rain.

Lampoon

In the modern vernacular, the lampoon is more "up-front-and-personal". Although seen in modern poetry, it has been around for some while and has always found favour when taking a shot at the high and the mighty - particularly those of regal birth or of a political persuasion.

In the past it was often seen as something simple and direct, which came and passed away quite quickly as time and the political environment changed and moved on.

The lampoon sought to expose some unfortunate individual to ridicule. It was, in effect, a verbal cartoon...often quite clever, and always amusing. Frequently it was the work of some noted person, although common sense suggested that it might be prudent for the poet to remain anonymous.

One famous exception would be John Wilmot (1647 - 1680) and his epitaph for Charles II:

> *Here lies a great and mighty king*
> *Whose promise none relied on.*
> *He never said a foolish thing,*
> *Nor ever did a wise one.*

Social Comment

Comedy in verse will often have a more general public appeal and may be best described as "poetry for the moment". Some current item of news or political situation (perhaps a recent scandal or ill-advised action by someone in the public eye) will invariably draw comment. In many ways, sources of modern communication (such as the internet) will rapidly propagate any such witty criticism, which may well be expressed in verse.

Local newspapers will often be happy to publish such items, and given the need to write within a tight time-frame (often just a few days) can serve as good training in the discipline of writing, helping to focus thoughts in a concise manner.

The following poem **"Shades o' Grey"** was written following the publication of an erotic romance novel "50 Shades of Grey" by E L James, which (I am told) featured some explicit sado-masochistic sexual practices, and achieved instant notoriety... as well as becoming an immediate best-seller. What, one wonders, might be the impact of such a book on a somewhat staid and slightly elderly couple Derbyshire?

As with the previous poem about **"Noah An' 'Is Ark"** (page 209), the use of phonetical spelling to indicate a particular dialect and thereby "place" the poem into a particular setting or environment can also provide added humour. I tend to favour the Derbyshire area for no better reason than having spent some time there, when the impact of both pronunciation and indeed the words themselves inspired many poems, both serious and less so, as the following example shows.

SHADES O' GREY

She said she wanted sex. 'e said it weren't like Saturday.
She said as 'ow she knew but they should do it anyway.
By 'eck 'e wur surprised an' wurn't reet certain what t'say.

"But we 'aven't 'ad us curry lass, like what we always do
"Aye...'appen so," says she, "Tis time fer tryin' summat new."

"I 'as me needs, thar knows," says she. "Wi' passion an' wi' fire."
"Tis time t'satiate yon wild an' uncontrolled desire."

"Thar needs t'tak' control wi' summat hot an' like reet great."
"A curry then?" says 'e. "Nay lad...thee needs t'dominate."

"Tis S&M nay M&S will get us on t'boil –
wi' ropes an' 'andcuffs, blindfolds too, an' candles like, an' oil."

"Thar needs t'tak' us lad t'places we 'ave never been."
"Thurs Blackpool, lass," says 'e.
"Nay...t'other places we've nay seen

an' naughty like, but fun...yon realm o' wildest fantasy,
wur thee can run amok an' 'ave thar wicked way wi' me.

"Tis all in't book wi' shades o' grey – thar need t'ave a read."
"Aye, reet enough lass," then says 'e, an' so it wur agreed.

But lackin' still in't ropes an' stuff fur action like on't bed
'e went t'shops an' then come 'ome wi' curry like instead.

PLAYING WITH WORDS

Limerick and Clerihew

We have already considered how, when seeking rhymes or wishing to set a poem in a particular time and place, it is sometimes necessary to write in a phonetical manner. This can make the writing and reading of a poem slightly more difficult, but with perseverance will enhance the poem with an added charm.

Any poet possessed of a keen sense of national pride may also wish to show this in a distinctive manner. This was evident, for example, in the work of many Scottish poets, even before the time of Robert Burns (1759 - 1796) although emulated by him.

The aim was to write poetry that included not only normal "English" words (spelt in a way to indicate a distinctive Scottish brogue), but also to intersperse these with words unique to the native tongue. For example, a "wee tim'rous beastie" could only live north of the border.

Performance poetry, which seeks to be heard rather than read (although one does not preclude the other) will also use dialect and accent to add emphasis to the poem.

Limerick

It is claimed that the limerick was originally of French derivation, although this is disputed. There is also a precedent in some English medieval poetry, such as "The Cuckoo Song", which has survived to modern times, and begins:

The summer is a-coming in,
and loudly sing cuckoo!
It grows the seed
and blows the mead,
and springs the wood anew.

As we know from our consideration of types of meter, the limerick is one of the relatively rare examples of the amphibracic meter. It has just five lines with lines 1,2 and 5 of three feet, and lines 3 and 4 with two feet.

The rhyme scheme is simply:

aabba

The limerick was popularised by Victorian poet Edward Lear (1812 - 1888), who tended to have the fifth line as a refrain of the first, although this is not necessary. The limerick is always amusing and frequently bawdy.. bordering on quite risqué topics.

Modern use has also seen the limerick form return to more serious topics, but the underlying appreciation of anticipated amusement generally predominates this form of poetry.

PABLO RUIZ

There was a young man, I am told,
With arms speckled cobalt and gold –
Vermillion hair,
Chinese white everywhere;
Picasso at work...six years old.

Clerihew

The clerihew is a form of light verse devised by Edmund Clerihew Bentley (1875-1956) and consists of a quatrain of two couplets:

aabb

It may be in any meter, although iambic meter is often preferred, and takes as its subject any well-known person. The clerihew may be satirical but is always amusing.

SHAKESPEARE

Shakespeare - he of sonnet fame
'tis said would rightwise spell his name
with variations seventeen...
which makes my spelling less obseen.

GERARD MANLEY HOPKINS

Gerard Manley Hopkins brings
a springing-sprung verse glorious for all dappled things,
but of a modern view, new uniformity and best
apples of a-speckle freckled frolic fail the Tesco test!

JOHN BETJEMAN

John Betjeman (departed now)
spoke once of bombs to fall on Slough.
Yet modern planners have it seems
fulfilled his wishes to extremes.

LONGFELLOW

From a poem by Longfellow –
melodrama song and mellow;
from the words of such an author
learnt we then of Hiawatha.

Rhopalic Verse, Cinquains and Triversian

The presentation of the poem on the page may also be dictated by the required construction of the poem itself, in terms of line-lengths as determined by syllable counts or the number of feet per line. There are several ways this may happen, as follows.

Rhopalic Verse

Rhopalic verse is a form in which each line is a metrical foot longer than the preceding line. Clearly this will have a limit, since lines of more than seven or eight feet tend to break down into shorter lengths.

In some instances, this effect may be reversed (there is no term for this) to reduce the poem back to its original short line length once more. See **"Misty Dawn Meadow"** (page 228).

Cinquains

The cinquain is a poem of five lines and was invented by Adelaide Crapsey (1878 - 1914). It is based on the Japanese tradition of counting syllables. For the cinquain, however, the lines are arranged with 2, 4, 6, 8 and finally 2 syllables. There is no requirement for rhyme or meter, although these can be introduced if an added challenge is required.

This allows a simple theme to be developed slowly and then finally brought to a sharp conclusion. The challenge, of course, is in developing the theme in so limited a number of words, which (as we shall see in the following chapter) is essentially what Japanese poetry is all about.

SOMETIMES

Sometimes
I think of you,
when skies grow dark with rain,
and I pause to look for rainbows...
sometimes

SO DARK

So dark
the night: this night
even the stars are lost
hidden by clouds, like sudden doubts
waiting

DAWN

Silence
comes with the dawn:
and pale with morning mist,
a gentle glow at the window
beckons

BLUEBELLS

Bluebells
mist the meadow
beneath a hazy sky –
blurring the edges of morning
once more.

DAYS PASS

Days pass –
warm summer brings
a sudden autumn chill
whispering of winter's beauty
so soon

AGAIN

Again...
begin again.
Rehearse the words once more
whilst hurrying quickly to school
So late!

Triversan

The triversan poem is made up from any number of triversan (three line) stanzas, which are usually written in the form of free verse and reliant on normal speech. Each line is a single phrase, and each stanza is a complete sentence. The poem that follows has a regular meter, and rhymes have been introduced for pairs of stanzas. It is also an allusion to the famous poem "The Road Not Taken" by Robert Frost (1874 - 1963).

A subtle reference to this original poem is given in the line "A mossy road once touched by frost..."

THE ROAD LESS TRAVELLED

There is a road less travelled by
that I, alas, have yet to find –
a road I may have passed that was not seen.

Though where this was, or how and why
some hidden way was left behind
I know not, nor of when this may have been.

A mossy road once touched by frost
and dappled sunshine in the spring –
some quiet lane that led another way

through yellow woods, to wander lost
upon a journey, which might bring
a difference to fill the bright, new day.

I know not where this road may be
although quite certain it lies near –
should I but just retrace a step or two.

A grassy road that waits for me
as yet untrodden, yet as clear
may lead to things once dreamed, left still to do.

ALL SHAPES AND SIZES

Spatial and Concrete Poetry

Spatial Poetry

Poetry has its roots in performance and will ever remain so, although a wider audience is now achieved through the medium of the printed word. One of the more interesting aspects of poetry is the flexibility by which it can be transformed into any visual or literary experiment. The way in which a poem sits on the page - it's spatial presentation, has therefore come to be significant, and may well enhance or reflect the subject of the poem itself.

A spatial poem can be presented on the page in one of two ways:

Concrete Poetry

Concrete poetry emerged experimentally during the early 1960s and concentrated mainly on presentation, often taking shape through the use of bold blocks of print. The use of different fonts and font sizes was frequently applied to amplify this effect.

This was very much a visual medium, and the poem itself was invariably quite brief and written in free verse. With the advent of modern printing methods and use of coloured illustrations, concrete poetry seems to have seen a decline in popularity in recent times.

```
     From the street
          and busy feet
               the steps
                 lead down
               below the town
                         to
                     hidden
                   basements
                 dark       below
                which         few
                men          know
               nor wish to go
```

Calligrammes

The calligramme is, effectively, an ordinary poem except for the way it is presented. This is made easier with modern technology, which may allow us to justify the poem to right or left, or present the poem symmetrically.

Other, more artistic arrangements, are possible so that, for example, a poem about a tree might have lines arranged to provide a silhouette of the tree. In some cases, colour can also add to this illusion, and clearly a poem written in free verse or blank verse would allow for a more artistic representation.

ACORN PROMISE

Slowly
and **majestically**
*a **slender** shoot of destiny*
that rises **slowly** from **the** fertile earth.
This miracle of a birth that ***reaches*** for the ***sky***
and ***climbing*** *high* **whilst** hidden in soft **golden** rings
seasons of past ***remembering*...**
This monument *of* **swaying** branch and **leaf**
that **builds** a canopy of green becoming gold
and naked to **the** *winter's cold.*
Seasons *of* ***past*** remembering:
the sun and *rain* with ***chill*** winds
blowing once *again*
Days without ***number***
times **of** slumber
sap
new
chapters
captured
joyfully.
This ***charm***
and *noble* ***majesty***
This *slender* shoot grown to a ***mighty*** tree.

TIME REFLECTION

                    I
                   am
                  new
                slowly
               growing
            opening my
          hidden secrets
        the perfumed heart
      of my beauty displayed
       before I begin to fade
        in the summer sun
         my petals slowly
          falling lost and
           soon to be
            forgotten
             slowly
              gone
               am
                I
                 I
                 am
                 grown
                 old with
                 harsh thorns
                 seeking to guard
                 against the reality of
                 what I have now become
                 and a final measure against
                 this vulnerability I feel
                 lost and neglected
                 with my former
                 beauty gone
                 forgotten
                 faded
                 ever
                 sad
                 am
                 I

Clearly, syllable counting can lend itself to the presentation of the poem in the form of a calligramme as will rhopalic verse with lines of increasing metric feet (see page 220).

For example:

MISTY DAWN MEADOW

    beyond the misty meadow
      hidden by hazy trees
       the sound of water
        a narrow stream
         cascading
          over
           stones
            the
           sparkle
          of sunlight...
         leafy shadows
        a stream of music
       echoing somewhere lost
      beyond the misty meadow

Found Poem

The poem that follows is also of a deliberate construction, yet might easily have originated as a "found" poem - one that is recognised as such although not intended by the writer at the time.

In this example, the poem is written to give the language expected of a newspaper report, and is presented as something that might have emerged from a newspaper column.

GIRL MURDERED

*a **g**irl has been found murdered
was e**i**ghteen years old and had
was desc**r**ibed as a brutal attack
along the o**l**d canal pathway has
no apparent **m**otive as yet though
described as a s**u**dden frenzy with
she was a pretty gi**r**l and had been
with samples of bloo**d** collected for
there has been a polic**e** appeal for
items although the murde**r** weapon
are still seeking clues in th**e** hope
of the public have been warne**d** to*

Vanishing Sonnet, Nonet and Minute

Vanishing Sonnet

Poems written where the number of syllables per line vary may also take on a distinctive shape by virtue of this restriction, and one such example is found in the modern form of a vanishing sonnet. Naturally we will expect the poem to have fourteen lines, and it will also have a count of fourteen syllables for the first line.

The challenge is then to reduce each successive line by one syllable, which naturally leaves just one syllable in the final line. The tapering shape of the poem is an inevitable consequence of this challenge, and can be exaggerated into a more precise shape by allowing additional spaces at intervals between the words.

The vanishing sonnet is usually written as free verse, and can draw a subject to a succinct close. As a rhyming sponnet this will invariably be in couplets, if only to allow the rhyme to become apparent.

VANISHING SONNET

The vanishing sonnet begins with a confident air –
counting the syllables: plenty remaining to share.
Taking the time... considering what words to write,
gifted with merit, fun and sense of delight.

It all begins well, whilst clearly aware
how the meter and rhyme are both there.
Moving along... getting it right
line after line growing tight.

Yet how often it seems
thoughts lingering still,
words are betrayed –
just like dreams
that will
fade.

Nonet

Constructed in much the same way as the vanishing sonnet, the nonet follows a similar construction of decreasing syllables - beginning with nine syllables in the first line and decreasing to just one in the final line. The preferred approach is to use free verse, but the more difficult use of rhyme (usually in couplets) is possible.

FAINT LIGHT

Many a time I begin to write:
a light that flickers late at night,
though unsure where this may lead.
Tempted then to proceed
with thoughts given voice...
some unknown choice.
Yet each word
clearly
heard.

Many a time... for it seems to be
I hear a whisper calling me,
and a time when I must write.
A time of true delight
and of poetry
I seem to see,
like a light
in the
night

Minute

One other modern form of poetry dependent on the counting of syllables is the minute. It takes its name from the fact that there are exactly sixty syllables in the poem, which is presented in twelve lines and a syllable count as shown

8 4 4 4 8 4 4 4 8 4 4 4

The poems may be divided into three stanzas to show this regular pattern, although it is more often written as a single stanza. The poem is also written in rhyming couplets...

a a b b c c ... and so on.

Non-rhyming versions are known, but this is generally seen as taking the easy route!

NO OCEAN GREEN

No ocean ever shone more green:
no sea was seen
more rippled bright
in morning light.

No turning tide of wave on wave
displayed more brave
some gentle sway
that summer's day.

No lake more lovelier revealed
than one broad field
of swaying corn
with beauty born

IN LOOKING BACK

In looking back, I thought that we
would always be
in love, aware
how we might share
our lives together constantly.
I did not see
it was not so —
how you would go.
I will remember once again
how in the rain
we said goodbye,
not knowing why.

Keeping Count

We know from examples of medieval poetry such as the kyrielle, that the counting of syllables is nothing new. We might even note that the standard iambic pentameter of a traditional sonnet will likewise have a regular ten syllables per line. It seems evident in modern poetry, particularly when written as non-rhyming free verse, that the syllabic verse will also have an appeal in lending some distinctive form of structure to the poem.

It is equally obvious that there may be any number of ways to achieve this. Normally a mathematical progression is preferred, as shown in the vanishing sonnet and nonet, although the subtlety of a regular "pattern" may be found in some forms, such as the aptly named minute poem of 60 syllables per stanza.

There is, of course, no reason to suppose that we might not invent our own format and use this to demonstrate an equal skill in the composition of a poem, so why not give it a try?

Etheree and Twin Etheree

Etheree

We might readily discover many more poems based on the counting of syllables, but will look at just one other example named after the inventor, Etheree Taylor Armstrong (1918 - 1994) a modern American poet. The etheree is a simple non-rhyming poem of ten lines with an increasing number of syllables per line beginning with one, which gives the appearance of something slowly opening out...

PYRAMID

*One...
then two,
leads to three
and so onward,
beginning to show
a form of construction,
although hardly demanding
nor giving any great challenge
yet having the distinct appearance
of some ancient Egyptian pyramid.*

Reverse Etheree

The etheree has hardly the appearance of anything radical, and the reverse etheree simply repeats the same format, beginning with ten syllables in the first line and decreasing, in much the same way as the vanishing sonnet, which we have already considered.

Double Etheree

The double etheree simply combines the two forms, and is usually shown as a single stanza non-rhyming poem of twenty lines, with syllables (1 to 10) and then reversed (10 to 1).

Twin Etheree

The development of the twin etheree is attributed to Robert Crockett, a contemporary American poet. It has twenty lines in rhyming couplets, with a progressive syllable count of 1,1,2,2...up to 10,10.

This gives a stepped appearance to the poem although the use of some single words of many syllables tends to disrupt this pattern, as seen in the example that follows. It will be found that the twin etheree has the effect of allowing the slow development of a theme.

COME... COME

Come...
come.
Let me
gently
find my way -
learn to say
the words sincere
you long to hear.
Come... come: walk with me.
Let us gracefully
discover all we share,
and so become aware
of all that love may reveal.
Come... come: let us learn to feel
whatever love we may then find
and likewise leave the past behind.
Begin again: face the bright new day,
hand in hand together...find our way.
Come, be my love, and let me love you too:
as lovers then to share in all we do.

A Final Count

There is a tendency when writing poems with a strict syllable count to focus on the mathematics of the construction, whilst losing sight of the greater importance in creating a poem of literary merit. The flow of words frequently mentioned in other forms of poetry should still be apparent, even when strictly inhibited by the poem's construction. It is, perhaps, necessary also to ask what is the aim of these modern forms of syllabic verse?

If, as is often the case, the aim is in the presentation, then returning to our original theme of "all shapes and sizes", we might do well to observe a more liberal attitude and allow some slight bending of the rules.

This is perhaps best demonstrated in the poem **"Time Reflection"** (page 227), where the number of syllables per line varies not only to maintain steady flow of words, but also to give the intended spatial shape of rose thorns.

ORIENTAL POETRY

Japanese Poetry

Whenever oriental poetry is mentioned, thoughts turn immediately to the haiku, a traditional form of Japanese poetry which has penetrated the western culture to an extent not matched by any other form of writing from the Far East. The apparent simplicity of the haiku, with just three lines and a minimum of words will have an immediate attraction, although this often belies the extreme skill necessary to write in this way.

There are, as we might expect, many forms of Japanese poetry. We will also examine poetry from other eastern countries, such as China and Korea. One critical point that needs to be made at the outset, however, is with regard to the problems that occur from any attempts at translation. We have only to consider difficulties arising from similar cultures when, for example, translating contemporary poems of French poet Charles Pierre Baudelaire (1821 - 1867) into English, to know how true is the maxim that "much may be lost in translation".

Consider then any similar attempt at understanding the work of Basho (1644 - 1694), who lived in a remote and alien culture (even by today's standards), and wrote in a style that we are only slowly coming to understand. Small wonder we find ourselves teetering on the edge of a chasm in our ability to fully comprehend the depth of such poetry. However, there is an empathy in our appreciation of what poetry... all poetry, must attempt to achieve, and we have time enough to come to see the beauty that awaits our discovery.

Japanese poetry is simple in construction and yet very precise in its nature. It is based on the precept of counting syllables, and has no regard to either rhyme or meter. All meaning to be derived from the poem must be contained within the poem itself, which explains why there are no titles given to such poems.

haiku (hokku)

Best known of all Japanese poetry, the haiku has three lines of alternating 5-7-5 syllables giving 17 syllables in total. The haiku should also capture an aspect of nature and allude to a season.

Beyond this, however, is the less tangible aspect which requires that the haiku should say more than is described in words. In many ways, the spaces between the words are of an importance equal to that of the words themselves. This depth may be achieved through a collection of brief glimpses and succinct expression, where the words serve to provide nuances of shade and emotion.

The use of metaphor should also allow the poem to work on several levels of understanding, allowing the reader to combine all of these elements into a larger comprehension of what is being said. All of this in just three lines!

the summer cornfield -
steel blades in a sea of gold
splattered with poppies

the candle flame dies
drowns within a pool of wax
smoke thickens the air

a pale autumn sun
plumbing the lake's deep secret
a final embrace

the book burns slowly
delicate fingers of flame
turning the pages

It may be noted that haiku and other forms of Japanese poetry usually lack punctuation, since this might imply a particular stress on some words. It is left to the reader to apply whatever pauses and emphases are necessary to achieve an individual understanding.

A more modern (predominantly western) use of haiku is when they are written as stanzas in a poem.

ACROSS THE RIVER

sharp pin-points of light
scattered across the river
from the falling rain

slow waters swirling
with wavering reflections
of the autumn trees

a breeze sends ripples
brushing across the water
at the river's turn

dark branches swaying
with the steady drip of rain
from whispering trees

leaves of gold and bronze
floating in the gentle air
like soft confetti

tanka (waka or uta)

The tanka is an extended form of the haiku. It begins with the same 5-7-5 syllable lines, followed by a pair of lines with 7 syllables. This gives us 31 syllables in total. The same brevity of expression, use of metaphor and layers of meaning expected of the haiku are implicit also in the tanka, together with some subtle reference to nature and the seasons.

The construction of the tanka is such that one subject is treated in the first two lines, with a second subject in the next two lines. The final line will then normally be a paraphrase of what has been already stated.

For example:

snow falls....suddenly
puncturing the dark landscape
soft speckles of white
like an unfinished picture
or badly printed postcard.

naga-uta (choka)

The naga-uta (choka) is a further extended form of the haiku, beginning with the 5-7-5 syllable lines, and then followed by any number of pairs of lines with 7-5 syllables. Theoretically, such a poem might extend to include a great number of lines, although in practice this is rarely so. The poem will always end with a couplet of two 7 syllable lines.

Typically, this gives line of 5-7-5-7-5-7-5....7-5-7-7 syllables

PHANTOM RAIN

the evening hushed
and beyond the balcony
dark shadows moving

banana plants stirred from rest
slow fluttering fans
the broad leaves softly swaying
sifting faint moonlight
through delicate shades of green

eyes closed - near to sleep
comes the sound of phantom rain
gently whispering again

LANDS END

here above the cliffs
where the dark sea is shredded
and torn into wisps
of salt spray and frayed water

here where rocks exist
as if necessary now
to define the sea
to challenge the erosion
of sand and ocean

here where time is held
obedient to purpose
some hidden design
and the deep infinity
which will determine
the metaphor of landscape

here is the promise
to decipher all meaning
the explanation
by which unending struggle
will be wrought into beauty

renga

The renga is a collective poem written by two poets over a period of time. It has five lines and the same appearance as a tanka, with lines of (5-7-5-7-7 syllables). However, it is composed differently. The first poet writes the first three lines and the second poet, having considered and reflected on what is effectively a haiku, will then add a couplet response.

renga chain

The renga chain begins with a renga, but is then passed on to other poets who add successive triplets and couplets to amplify or comment on the first (haiku) triplet. This can become quite complex on an intellectual level, and may continue over many stanzas and many months.

haiku no renga

Haiku no renga is applied to a humorous renga chain and takes its name from haiku of humour.

senryu

The senryu form was developed by the Japanese poet Senryu Karai (1718 – 1790). It is of the same construction as haiku, with the same use of language and levels of meaning through metaphor, but takes human activities as its subject matter rather than nature. This may often include some amusing aspect of human behaviour or deeper emotional tone.

For example:

> *a box of old nails*
> *all sizes and all rusty*
> *and every one bent*

Modern Haiku

It is known that attempts to translate ancient Japanese haiku will inevitably result in some slight loss. Many of the more famous Japanese haiku date from a time and culture radically different from any comparable experience in western society. This, combined with the extreme succinctness and use of minimum words to provide a profound depth and meaning, is a challenge in itself.

This is particularly true if a translation is also made in an attempt to retain the strict arrangement of three lines with syllables of 5-7-5.

To overcome this, some of the more recent translations have forfeited the structure of 5-7-5 syllables in order to achieve a better meaning. Whether this is wholly successful is a matter of debate, although it has resulted in a relaxation of the traditional haiku construction.

There is also an argument which suggests that the more succinct the haiku, the greater the weight of the words. This has evolved into forms of modern haiku being written with a variable number of syllables per line, and even a variation in the number of lines.

Whilst this would seem to undermine the basic concept of traditional haiku, many modern writers prefer to wander away from the original and somewhat well-worn pathway.

some girls I have loved
others
I have understood

I will not wave goodbye
in the rain she said
waving

green trees
so far from the city
so green

the contrast of a grey stone wall
and scarlet painted door
the stone-grey grey

Chinese Poetry

Chinese poetry is a very visual form, which requires the presentation of Chinese characters in precise vertical and horizontal positions. The characters might represent a single word or short phrase. In this way, the phrases are reflected by those in adjacent spaces, and whilst the poem is read in a normal manner (vertically in Chinese) some regard is made to the corresponding horizontal meanings.

Clearly, any western translation of such an arrangement is virtually impossible, and such translations as have been made tend to rely on the achievement of succinct expression – what we might otherwise describe as a "pen-picture".

Chinese poetry will also include a reference to nature and the seasons, with an expression of such beauty through the interaction with human emotions. This results in quite brief poems of great depth.

t'ang

Chinese poetry reached a peak during the T'ang dynasty (618-907), when all forms were adopted and refined. Ancient Chinese poems were usually composed of lines of four characters, with occasional rhyme, although this varied. New types of poetry were introduced during the reign of Emperor Wu (140-87 BC) with five or seven characters.

shi or shih was a general term used for all types of poetry or poems.

ku-shih (ancient style) had rules, but these were not mandatory and allowed the poet freedom to write. One such poet of this period, Li Po, also known as Li-Bai (712 -770 AD) wrote in the ku-shih style.

lü-shih (regulated verse) consisted of eight lines of five or seven syllables, with fine distinctions in tonal quality.

jinti-shi

Jinti-shi is a Chinese term which literally means "modern-form poetry" and refers to a regulated style of poetry that developed from the 5th century onwards. The jinti-shi employs four tones: the level tone and three deflecting tones (rising, falling and entering). Tu Fu (712 - 770 AD) was the most accomplished exponent of jinti-shi during the Tang dynasty.

tz'u

Towards the end of the t'ang period a new verse form developed known as tz'u. This broke away from formal construction (shih), allowing irregular lengths of lines up to eleven syllables, and in order to be more readily understood was written in the natural rhythms of normal speech.

xin-shi

Shi and shih are western interpretations of the Chinese characters 詩 or 诗. This is a very modern Chinese term which means literally "new poetry". A greater degree of freedom is allowed, although concern with concise expression is paramount.

> ***BRINGING RAIN***
>
> *a thin grey blanket of cloud*
> *unrolls across the lake*
> *bringing rain*
>
> *jagged ripples*
> *lapping at the muddy bank*
> *where tall reeds softly sway*

SOMEWHERE UNSEEN

tonight the pale moon hides
shy and unseen

shrouded by a veil of cloud
a gossamer of pearly grey

and somewhere dark and heavy
comes the rumble of thunder

the rustle of autumn leaves
stirring in the night
a chill breeze passing through.

Korean Poetry

Korean poetry is also concerned with the counting of syllables and use of terse expression to portray greater depths of meaning. Traditionally, the poetry is usually written in three lines, but will include a greater number of syllables than is found in Japanese haiku and the like. Some reference to nature and the seasons must also to be included.

Sijo Verse

Sijo verse is a form that dates from a time of great antiquity. It includes three lines: the first two composed of either 14 or 15 syllables, and the last composed of 15 syllables. Clearly any western attempt at this format can result in lines of such extraordinary length that they may ultimately be broken down into shorter phrases, although as examples show it is still possible to retain the required structure in three lines:

WIND CHIMES

wind chimes caressed by a morning breeze sing of their pleasure:
the soft gleam of sunlight with a faint stirring brings harmony
echoing... echoing gently through the magical garden

RETURNING HOME

returning home pausing to see the setting of the sun
as it sinks slowly into a sea of soft marshmallow clouds:
a moment alone with my thoughts and a poem lingering

NEW BEGINNING

high in the oak tree a sparkle of sunlight on wrinkled limbs
heavy with ancient knowledge and the fresh-green leaves of spring:
the old and the new whilst a thrush sings of a new beginning

FINAL WORDS

Final words

The Amateur Poet

An amateur is defined as someone fond of doing something and cultivating this activity as a pastime, which will find favour with most of us who have an interest in writing poetry.

Unfortunately, a modern meaning of the word amateur is that of someone who does a thing in a slip-shod or untrained manner.

Whilst we choose to write poetry as a hobby, this should not imply any poor attempt at writing, or that our efforts are not taken seriously!

An Amazing Journey

Stephen John Fry (1957 -) once said:

"Poetry is the language in which man explores his own amazement."

Inevitably, therefore, writing poetry can be a very private undertaking, in which the poet may observe, meditate and finally write on some aspect of life.

This approach may also be reflected in the way the poem is personally expressed, even when the experience or observation described arises from of an empathy with events and emotions, and is not a confessional experience of them. It is a common assumption that anything written in the first person must relate to some direct experience, which is not always so.

IF DAYS ARE DARK

If, at times, the world becomes a troubled place –
  a time of sad confusion and uncertain grace.
If days in dull procession follow long and grey,
  with lack of true direction found along the way.

If faint ambition dwells where hope has disappeared,
  and nothing of tomorrow shows the clouds have cleared.
If dark despair floods in to fill all that you think,
  and it appears you stand upon the chasm's brink.

If there is nothing you may find to feel or love:
  no bright new challenge you might wish to rise above.
If this is so – then do not seek for cause or rhyme:
  nor expectation of some sudden change in time.

Yet look instead to find a gentle place to be,
  gifted with peace and nature's quiet remedy.
And though the days seem dark as night – look for a star,
  and in that certain light remember who you are.

Getting It Right

A knowledge of English grammar - even the simple ability to spell words correctly - is essential if we are to write poetry that will be taken seriously and have some literary merit. It has not been the intention of this book to provide an education in English, although we have looked at certain aspects such as punctuation and the need to communicate our thoughts in a precise and direct manner.

One other aspect when writing poetry is an ability to place the poem within a time-frame. Are we thinking of the past, the present or the future? Are our thoughts determined, pensive or uncertain? This will have a direct effect on the poem, and is achieved primarily through the selection of verbs and verb tenses.

The following and final poem "**Tense Times**" is a light-hearted illustration of these various nuances of expression.

As was mentioned in the introduction to the book, the aim is to communicate our thoughts in an honest and original manner: to strike a chord with the reader. It is obvious that what we write will arise not only from what we see, but how this relates to our former experiences.

The same is true of the reader, who will draw from a poem what relates to his or her own experiences. No poem will ever convey the same meaning to everyone. However, the one essential aspect for the poet is to write with an emotional honesty. This will shine through the poem and elevate the words to a greater level of understanding.

The spark of inspiration necessary when writing poetry cannot be taught. As was said at the outset, the best that this book might hope to achieve will be to help broaden and enhance an inherent skill.

Where rules exist, it is as well always to remind ourselves that these should assist in what we want to express, and never constrict the flow of words. Rules are at best a guiding pathway, and we should never lack courage if we decide to wander off this track, whenever we feel the need to do so.

Who knows what may await us, hidden beyond the trees?

Toby Wren
July 2015

TENSE TIMES

Beginning here **I write** *within the <u>present simple</u> tense.*
I might say **I do write,** *since either way it still makes sense.*
Although if the <u>continuous present</u> aspect is made clear,
then I would hope that you may see how **I am writing** *here.*

Now in the <u>present perfect</u> **I have written** *something too*
from which you may assume that this is what I like to do,
and for a while **I have been writing** *in a simple rhyme*
throughout a <u>present perfect and continuous</u> length of time.

At one time in the <u>simple past</u> - known as the <u>preterite,</u>
I wrote *or* **I did write** *myself a poem ...something bright.*
Yet had I thought to pause and briefly spoken, then I might
in an <u>imperfect past</u> have simply said **I used to write.**

It seems that a <u>continuous past</u> will somehow reconcile
how **I was writing** *(which at least was true for just a while).*
A <u>conditional</u> awareness found in actions and well-meant...
how **I would write** *if then inspired by all that came and went.*

In the <u>pluperfect,</u> or <u>past perfect</u> days that I have known
when **I had written** *many poems quietly alone,*
I had been writing, *although never really knowing why*
how a <u>continuous, past perfect</u> time had passed me by.

In the <u>future</u> I know **I will write** *without a doubt –*
since writing is, in fact, what all of this has been about.
A new and <u>future perfect,</u> which will likewise then reveal
of how **I will have written** *many things I truly feel.*

A <u>continuous future</u> waits ahead and clearly seems to be
I will be writing *for a while, since I can plainly see*
a <u>future perfect and continuous</u> time without delay
when **I will have been writing,** *and still finding things to say.*

INDEX

ALPHABETICAL INDEX OF POEMS

Poems are arranged in alphabetical order and include page numbers as well as references showing topics that the poems are intended to illustrate.

Title	Page	Reference
A Gathering Of Dreams	161	Modern sonnet (mixed meter)
A New Wren Sonnet	160	Wren sonnet (acrostic)
A Quiet Neet In	189	Modern Ode, dialect, comedy,
A Rusted Hook	133	Sestet (abcabc)
A Simple Verse	41	Envelope stanza, mixed meter
A Summer's Day	171	Ballade royal (adaddcC)
A Winter's Day	132	Sestet (ababab)
Absolute Need	128	Triversan (3-line) free verse
Across The River	241	Japanese haiku stanzas
Acorn Promise	226	Calligramme poem
Adlestrop Denied	84	Allusion poem (ababb)
Adlestrop In Winter	85	Allusion sestet (aab, ccb)
Again	221	Cinquain
And So It Is	80	Serpentine verse, refrain lines
Arrival Roundelay	178	Roundelay
As Before	138	Ballade (ababbcbcb)
At The Close Of Day	79	Repetition, random rhyme
At The Start	112	Paeon meter, couplets, comedy
Augured Graces	146	Random rhyme
Autumn Confetti	204	Alphabetical verse
Autumn Now	158	Terza rima sonnet
Autumn Sun	240	Japanese haiku
Ballad Of Life	167	Ballad (abab)
Beacons Of Happiness	39	Dactylic meter
Beauty	21	Prose poem
Bien Dans Sa Peau	102	Iambic octometer, Macaronic verse
Bluebells	221	Cinquain
Blue Tit Greeting	110	Couplets (aabb)
Books In Boxes	121	Terzain, triplet (aaa,bbb...)
Box Of Nails	244	Japanese senryu

Title	Page	Form
Brighton Days (Of Sun And Sunshine)	89	Pastiche, random rhyme, trochaic
Bringing Rain	247	Chinese xin-shi
Burning Book	240	Japanese haiku
Candle Flame	240	Japanese haiku
C'est Comme C'est	207	Macaronic verse (mixed languages)
Codicil	69	Leonine verse (mid-line rhymes)
Come... Come	235	Twin etheree, couplets
Coming Of The Rain	47	Paeon meter, couplets
Costly Christmas	71	Echo verse
Dawn	221	Cinquain
Dawn Darkness	184	Curtal sonnet (abcabcdbcdc)
Dawn Rising	109	Terza rima, refrain lines
Days Pass	221	Cinquain
Days That Pass	136	Rhyme royal (ababbcc)
December Days	70	Softened random rhyme
Dedicated Athletes	71	Echo verse
Deeds Done Well	62	Paeon meter (abaab)
Departure	44	Amphibrachic meter
Divided By Time	77	Consonance, comedy, couplets
Double Trouble	93	English language - plurals
Drowning Man	36	Mixed meter (abccab)
Dumb Beasts	149	Shakespearean sonnet
Dusk	117	Envelope stanzas (abba)
Epiphora	80	Epiphora (repeated words)
Eucalyptus Memory	191	Elegy
Everlong	157	Gerard Manley Hopkins sonnet (sprung verse)
Faint Light	231	Nonet (9-lines) syllable counting
Farmyard Corner	76	Assonance & alliteration
Fast Flying Feet	66	(abc,abc)
Fireside Thoughts	141	Pararhyme (consonant rhyme)
First Of The Few	45	Spencer stanza (ababbcbcc) Mixed meter, mixed rhyme
Five Acre Field	130	Refrain lines (Abccb, Adeed..)
Forty Years Ago	180	Triolet (ABaAabAB), wordplay
Fowey Harbour	58	Random (envelope) rhyme (ab cde cde ab)

From The Street	225	Concrete poetry
Frustration	108	Refrain lines
Garden Time	127	Terza rima sonnet
Geography Of Understanding	22	Free verse
Gerard Manley Hopkins	219	Clerihew
Ghosts	202	Double acrostic
Girl Murdered	229	Calligramme, found poetry
Ghostly Vowels	72	Vowel rhymes
Girls	245	Modern (Western) haiku
Goodbye	245	Modern (Western) haiku
Goosey, Goosey Gander	19	Nursery rhyme
Green Sanctuary	57	Free verse
Green Trees	245	Modern (Western) haiku
Grey On Grey	119	Paired stanzas (abcd, abcd)
Grey Stone Wall	245	Modern (Western) haiku
Happy In My Time	196	Welsh verse - Awdl Gywydd
Here With Me	140	Triolet (ABaAabAB)
How Easy It Was	26	Free verse
How So?	134	Sesta rima (ababcc)
Ice And Fire	177	Roundelay, refrain lines
If Days Are Dark	254	Mixed meter, couplets
If Fame Be Ours	142	Wren stanza (abcbacbca)
If It Comes To Be	55	Irregular meter and line lengths Envelope stanzas
If You Love Me	175	Roundel ([Ra]baR bab abaR)
In Looking Back	233	Minute (12-line, counting syllables)
In Search Of Rhyme	65	Spelling rhyme
In The Passing Of The Days	106	Refrain lines (ababa)
January	156	Modern sonnet (abc abc def def gg)
Jersey Celebration	122	Terzain, triplet rhymes (aaa, bbb...)
John Betjeman	219	Clerihew
Journey Onward	131	Linked refrain lines
Jubilation	201	Telestich, acrostic
Knowing	31	Mixed meter (abab)
Knowing Now	143	Ballade ten-line (ababbccdcd)
Known By Cats	114	Modern sonnet, refrain lines
Kyrielle Of Spring	185	Kyrielle (abaB cbcB dbdB)

Lai	187	*Lai*
Land's End	243	*Japanese naga-uta*
Last Of The Days	78	*Random rhyme, repetition,*
Limerick Rhyme	44	*refrain*
Lady... Fair Lady	40	*Amphibrachic meter*
Longfellow	219	*Dactylic meter*
Love Long Ago	176	*Clerihew*
Love Story	200	*Rondelet (AbAabbA)*
		Use of metaphor, sestet paired
Lovers We Were	153	*stanzas (abacca, dbdeed)*
Love's Last Farewell	169	*Shakespearean sonnet*
Loves Many Shared	155	*Ballade (ababbcbc)*
Lunacy	135	*Spenser sonnet*
Metric Wit	50	*7-line stanzas*
Ming Kung Chen	64	*Meters (7 types)*
Misty Dawn Meadow	228	*Dialect, comedy*
Moments Lost	186	*Calligramme, syllable counting*
Moving On	151	*Kyrielle (abaB cbcB dbdB)*
Nasturtiums	152	*Shakespearean sonnet*
		Shakespearean sonnet (modern)
		iambic heptameter
Never Mine	144	*Roundelay*
New Beginning	249	*Korean sijo verse*
New York – New Shoes	54	*Irregular meter (abab)*
Night Magic	33	*Iambic meter (aab, ccb)*
No Ocean Green	232	*Minute (12-line, counting*
Noah An' 'Is Ark	209	*syllables) Ode, comedy, dialect*
Octopus Puzzle	92	*Words, language, comedy*
Odeless	175	*Roundel ([Ra]baR bab abaR)*
Old Age And New Days	100	*Sonnet, (abcabc, defdef, gg)*
Ourtime	94	*Pastiche, word-play, comedy*
Over Ocean Depths	107	*Spenser stanzas, refrain*
Pablo Ruiz	218	*Limerick, amphibrachic meter*
Pantoum Of Time	182	*Pantoum,*
		interlocked refrain lines
Pantoum Of Love	183	*Pantoum, interlocked refrain*
		lines
Pebbles	125	*Terza rima (aba, bcb, cdc...)*
Phantom Rain	242	*Japanese naga-uta*

Prosody	66	Vowel rhyme, refrain
Pyramid	234	Etheree (syllable count), free verse
Quatorzain	162	Quatorzain (random rhyme sonnet)
Red Dragons	195	Welsh verse - Awdl Gywydd
Reflections By A Pond	161	Modern sonnet, variable meter
Resolution	68	Random rhyme
Returning Home	249	Korean sijo verse
Robbery	123	Terzain, linked triplets (abb, acc...)
Sapphic Ambition	120	Sapphic stanza
Sea View Rubaiyat	116	Rubaiyat (aaba, bbcb, ccdc...)
Shades o' Grey	213	Comedy, dialect
Shakespeare	219	Clerihew
Sid	43	Limerick, amphibrachic meter
Silent Fields	126	Terza rima (aba, bcb,) enjambment
Sings The Robin	165	Ballad
Small Wonder	20	Free verse
Snow Falls	242	Japanese tanka
So Dark	221	Cinquain
Somewhere Unseen	248	Chinese xin-shi
Sometimes	221	Cinquain
Sonnet Of Autumn	83	Shakespearean sonnet, assonance and alliteration
Sonnet Of Silver Fire	154	Petrarchian sonnet, assonance
Spenser Rhyme	141	Spenserian stanza (ababbcbcc)
Strangers	101	Iambic heptameter, couplets
Summer Cornfield	240	Japanese haiku
Summer Skies	59	Villanelle
Tarot	203	Compound acrostic
Tense Times	256	Language, grammar
The Poet's Gift	145	Shakespearean sonnet
The Poor Bird	25	Doggerel
The Road Less Travelled	222	Allusion, pastiche, triversan, linked stanzas (abc, abc)
The Silver Sea	75	Alliteration (-a-a)
The Turning Of The Seasons	49	Paeon meter, couplets

The Way Of Things	23	*Free verse*
Though We Are Grown Old	37	*Anapaestic meter, couplets*
Time Reflection	227	*Calligramme, Rhopalic verse*
Truth Unspoken	139	*Triolet stanza (AbaAabAB)*
Unimportant Things	137	*Ottava rima (abababcc)*
Valentine Rhyme	82	*Shakespearean sonnet, archaic language, acrostic*
Vanishing Sonnet	230	*modern sonnet, counting syllables*
Vidi Finem Belli Mortuos	164	*modern sonnet, variable meter*
Villanelle Rhyme	181	*Villanelle, use of refrain lines*
Voilà Tout	206	*Macaronic verse (mixed languages)*
What Words Are These ?	205	*Logaoedic (mixed meter)*
Where Shadows Grow	159	*Terza rima sonnet*
Where Sings The Wren	113	*Ballad stanza (-a-a)*
Wind Chimes	249	*Korean sijo verse*
Wine	176	*Rondelet (AbAabbA), comedy*
Woburn Walk	87	*Allusion, envelope stanzas (abccba)*
Words Remaining Here	144	*Roundelay*
Worry A Little If You Must	129	*Five-line stanzas (ababb)*

METERS SUMMARY LIST

Many forms of poetry depend on the use of a clearly defined meter. This does more than simply link the words together, but may also impart some particular quality to the mood or comprehension of a poem. The use of meter originated with the ancient Greeks, who employed a great number of which only a few have found their way into modern poetry.

In English poetry, the use of mixed meter may achieve an effect reminiscent of ancient Greek poetry, through the arrangement of stressed and unstressed syllables. The following list is a brief summary of most known types of meter, together with page references where further discussion and elaboration have been included in this book. The convention of (**TUM**-ty) is used once more to illustrate stressed and unstressed syllables.

Iambic		(ti-**TUM**)	32
		the **moon** shone **bright**	
Anapaestic		(ti-ti-**TUM**)	35
		we will **go** on our **way**	
Trochaic		(**Tum**-ti)	38
		gently **sing**ing	
Dactylic		(**TUM**-ti-ty)	39
		carefully **whisp**ering	
Monosyllabic (pause)		(**TUM**)	42
		he had come **late** in the night	
Amphibrachic		(ti-**TUM**-ty)	43
		what**ev**er sug**gest**ions	
Paeon	1st	(**TUM**-ti-ti-ty)	46
		dangerously **nav**igating	
	2nd	(ti-**TUM**-ti-ty)	46
		ac**cord**ing to the **weath**erman	
	3rd	(ti-ti-**TUM**-ty)	46
		disap**pear**ing in the **moon**light	
	4th	(ti-ti-ti-**TUM**)	46
		parti**cipate** in this de**bate**	
Anacrusis		(ti)	51
		slowly onward <u>and</u> forward	

Spondee		(***TUM-TUM***)	52
		the race began, **stop watch** in hand	
Pyrrhic		(*ti-ti*)	52
		coming *like a* ghost at twilight	
Tribrachic		(*ti-ti-ty*)	
		moments *in-between* arrival	
Diambic		(*ti-**TUM**-ti-**TUM***)	
		the ode *attributed* to Greeks	
Ditrochaic		(***TUM**-ti-**TUM**-ty*)	
		turning slowly ***anticlock***wise	
Tetrabrach		(*ti-ti-ti-ty*)	
		really *it isn't so* easy he said	
Molossus		(***TUM-TUM-TUM***)	
		the deputy was **shot down dead**	
Dispondee		(***TUM-TUM-TUM-TUM***)	
		come, come, don't wait	
Bacchic		(*ti-**TUM-TUM***)	
		the **hour glass** showed **time lost**	
Antibacchic		(***TUM-TUM**-ty*)	
		where the tall **greenbri**ers grow	
Amphimacer		(***TUM**-ti-**TUM***)	
		he flew the plane **up**side-**down**	
Choriambic		(***TUM**-ti-ti-**TUM***)	
		up and **away** over the **top**	
Antispastic		(*ti-**TUM-TUM**-ty*)	
		he played the drums **in*cessant*t**ly	
Ionic	Greater Ionic	(***TUM-TUM**-ti-ty*)	
		she knew about **seismol**ogy	
	Lesser Ionic	(*ti-ti-**TUM-TUM***)	
		Windsor Palace *was a ***great place***	
Epitrite	1st	(*ti-**TUM-TUM-TUM***)	
		she always was *his* **one true love**	
	2nd	(***TUM**-ti-**TUM-TUM***)	
		see the **big ship** sailing yonder	
	3rd	(***TUM-TUM**-ti-**TUM***)	
		one, two and **three**	
	4th	(***TUM-TUM-TUM**-ty*)	
		do not dawdle, **come back quick**ly	

GENERAL INDEX – KEY WORDS

accent (words)	27, 97
acrostic	81, 160, 199
double acrostic	202
compound acrostic	202
alcaics	193
amphibrachic (see meter)	43, 218
anacrusis (see meter)	51
anapaestic (see meter)	35
archaic words	81
Alexandrine	100, 140
alliteration	74, 157
allusion	83, 86, 208
alphabetical verse	203
archaic language	28, 36, 81
assonance	74, 157
Awdl Gywydd: Welsh verse	194
ballads & ballades:	165
ballad	113, 166
ballade	167
double ballade	170
ballade royal	136, 170
ballade supreme	172
double ballade supreme	172
standard ballade	168
blank verse	18, 22
calligramme poetry	226
cento	88
Chinese poetry:	246
t'ang, shi, shih, ku-shi, lü–shih	246
tz'u, jinti-shi, xin-shi	247
cinquains	220
Clerihew verse	218
cliché	77, 95
comedy verse (see also parody, pastiche, lampoon)	208
concrete poetry	225
consonance	75
couplets	25, 110

curtal sonnet	158, 184
dactylic (see meter)	39
dialect	63, 212, 217
doggerel	18, 24
echo verse	71
eight-line stanza ballade	138
elegy	190
enjambment	121, 166
envelope stanza	56, 117
envoy	166
epic	190
epiphora	79
etheree, reverse etheree, double etheree,	234
twin etheree	235
foot, feet (lines)	32, 98
found poem	20, 228
free verse(vers libre)	18, 56, 60, 128
grammar	25, 61, 96, 254, 256
Greek poetry	193
haiku (traditional) - see Japanese poetry	98, 239
haiku (modern) - see Japanese poetry	245
heroic line, couplet, stanza	100
hyperbole	96
iambic (see meter)	32
internal rhyme	69
inversion	25, 61
Japanese poetry:	98, 239
haiku (hokku)	240
haiku no renga	244
modern haiku	245
naga-uta (choka)	242
renga, renga chain	243
senryu	244
tanka (waka or uta)	241
Korean poetry: sijo verse	249
kyrielle	185
logaoedic poetry (mixed meter)	51, 56, 98, 205

lai	186
lampoon	88, 211
language: use of English	90, 91, 94
modern use	25, 63, 90, 94
use of tenses	256
languages: mixed (macaronic)	102, 206
Leonine verse (mid-line rhyme)	69
limerick	43, 217
line stress	27, 56
lines: lengths	97, 99
measurement (feet)	98
names	99
heroic	100
alexandrine	100, 140
litotes	96
macaronic verse (mixed languages)	102, 206
metaphor	20, 35, 199, 240
meter	32
meters: Greek forms : summary	265
meters: masculine (strong)	35, 48, 62
feminine (soft)	38, 62
irregular	53
mixed (logaoedic)	51, 56, 98, 205
meters : types	32, 50
amphibrachic	43, 218
anacrusis	51
anapaestic	35
iambic	22, 32
dactylic	39
paean, paeon	46, 62
pyrrhic	52
spondee	52
trochaic	38
monosyllabic pause	42
metonymy	95
minute	232
nonet	231

nursery rhymes	19
odes: Horation & Pindaric	188
odes: modern	189
onomatopoeia	96
oriental poetry	237
ottavo rima (see stanza forms)	137
paeon, paean (see meter)	46, 62
pantoum	182
pararhyme	66
parody	88, 208
pastiche	38, 88, 208
pauses (meter)	30
pen picture	21, 246
performance poetry	42, 56, 63, 73, 111
personification	95
plagiarism	83, 86, 208
poetic licence	29, 36
poetry	17
prose	18, 21
punctuation	30
puns	94, 202
pyrrhic (see meter)	52
quatorzain (see sonnet forms)	162
Queen's English	63
random rhyme	58, 67
refrain lines	24, 106, 165, 182
refrain: random	108
repetition	78
Rhopalic verse	220
rhyme forms:	
echo verse	71
masculine & feminine	35, 38, 62
phonetic (true) rhyme	63, 72
para-rhyme	66
random rhyme	58, 67
spelling rhyme	65
consonant rhyme	66
vowel rhyme	66

rondels, rondeaus, roundels, rondelets & roundelays :	173
rondel	173
rondeau	173
ten-Line rondeau	174
rondeau redouble	174
roundel	174
rondelet	176
roundelay	143, 177
rhyme royal (see stanza forms)	136
rhythm	56
rubai (rubaiyat)	115
rules (of poetry)	34, 59, 105, 152, 160
Sapphic verse (see stanza forms)	120, 193
septet (see stanza forms)	135
serpentine verse	80
sesta rima (see stanza forms)	134
sestet (see stanza forms)	132
sestina	191
Sicilian octave (see stanza forms)	137
sonnets	32, 145, 149
sonnet forms:	145
English or Shakespearean	145, 150
Gerard Manley Hopkins	157
Italian or Petrarchian	145, 153
Milton	155
mixed meter	160
modern	156
quatorzain	162
Spencer	145, 154
terza rima	145, 158
vanishing	230
Wilfred Owen	156
Wren	159
sonnet sequence	163
sonnet of sonnets	163
spatial poetry	225
Spenserian stanza (see stanza forms)	108, 140

spondee (see meter)	52
spoof	88, 208
sprung verse	52, 157
stanzas	105, 118
stanzas forms:	105
ballad	113, 166
ballade	167
couplets	25, 110
eight-line	138
envelope	56, 117
five-line	129
heroic	100
irregular rhymes	40
mixed lengths (random rhyme)	146
ottava rima	137
rubai (rubaiyat)	115
rhyme royal	136
Sapphic	120, 193
seven-line, septet	135
Sicilian octave	137
six-line, sestet	132
sesta rima	134
sonnet	145
Spenserian	108, 140
ten-line	142
tercets	180
triolet	139, 179
triplet, terzain	120
terza rima	124
triversan	127, 221
Venus and Adonis	134
Wren	142
stress (lines)	27, 56, 97
syllables	28, 97
syllables: counting	185, 228, 230
synecdoche	95
telestich poetry	201

tenses: types and use	256
tercets (see stanza forms)	180
terza rima (see stanza forms)	124
terza rima sonnet (see sonnet forms)	145, 158
terzain (see stanza forms)	120
translation (of poetry) (see also macaronic verse)	102, 206, 239
triolet	139, 179
triplet (see stanza forms)	120
triversan (see stanza forms)	127, 221
trochaic (see meter)	38
vanishing sonnet	230
Venus and Adonis (see stanza forms)	134
verse libre (free verse)	18, 56, 60, 128
verse	17
villanelle	59, 180
vowel (sounds)	73
Welsh verse: Awdl Gywydd	194
word accent	27
words: play on words	94, 179, 201
Wren stanza (see stanza forms)	142
Wren sonnet (see Sonnet forms)	159

POET REFERENCES
In alphabetical order

Guittone d'Arezzo	1235 - 1294	153
Etheree Taylor Armstrong	1918 - 1994	234
Basho	1644 - 1694	239
Charles Pierre Baudelaire	1821 - 1867	239
Edmund Clerihew Bentley	1875 - 1956	218
John Betjeman	1906 - 1984	219
Edmund Charles Blunden	1896 - 1974	66
Robert Burns	1759 - 1796	63, 217
Adelbert von Chamisso	1781 - 1838	182
Geoffrey Chaucer	1343 - 1400	65, 111, 167
Samuel Taylor Coleridge	1772 - 1834	17, 46
Adelaide Crapsey	1878 - 1914	220
Robert Crockett		235
Henri de Croi	15th century	167
Arnaut Daniel	1180 - 1200	191
Edward FitzGerald	1809 - 1883	115
Robert Lee Frost	1874 - 1963	20, 83, 115, 221
Stephen John Fry	1957 -	253
Gerard Manley Hopkins	1844 - 1889	52, 157, 158, 184, 205, 219
Senryu Karai	1718 - 1790	244
John Keats	1795 - 1821	188
Omar Khayyám	1048 - 1131	115
Edward Lear	1812 - 1888	218
Giaromo da Lentini	13th century	149
Leo	13th century	69
Li Po (Li Bai)	712 - 770	246
Henry Wadsworth Longfellow	1778 - 1850	38, 89, 219
Walter de la Mare	1873 - 1956	83
John Edward Masefield	1878 - 1967	42
William Topaz McGonagall	1825 - 1902	18
Roger McGough	1937 -	94
John Milton	1608 - 1674	155, 190, 193
Wilfred Owen	1894 - 1918	156
Francesco Petrarch	1304 - 1374	145, 153
Arthur Rimbaud	1854 - 1891	18, 60

Adenès Le Roi	1258 - 1297	179
Sappho	625BC - 570BC	120, 193
William Shakespeare	1564 - 1616	81, 134, 145, 149, 219
Percy Bysshe Shelley	1792 - 1822	188
Edmund Spenser	1552 - 1599	140, 145, 154
Algernon Charles Swinburne	1837 - 1909	174
Alfred Lord Tennyson	1809 - 1892	193
Dylan Marlais Thomas	1914 - 1953	195
Edward Thomas	1878 - 1917	83, 84
William Carlos Williams	1883 - 1963	127
John Wilmot	1647 - 1680	211
William Wordsworth	1770 - 1850	188
Toby Wren	1943 -	142, 159
Sir Thomas Wyatt	1503 - 1542	153
Tu Fu	712 - 770	247
William Butler Yates	1865 - 1939	86